James G. Kelly, PhD
Anna V. Song, MA, BA
Editors

Six Community Psychologists Tell Their Stories: History, Contexts, and Narrative

Six Community Psychologists Tell Their Stories: History, Contexts, and Narrative has been co-published simultaneously as *Journal of Prevention & Intervention in the Community*, Volume 28, Numbers 1/2 2004.

Pre-publication REVIEWS, COMMENTARIES, EVALUATIONS . . .

"SHOULD BE REQUIRED READING FOR ANY STUDENT aspiring to become a community psychologist as well as for practicing community psychologists interested in being provided unparalleled insights into the personal stories of many of the leading figures within our field. This book provides readers with an inside look at the reasons why a second generation of community psychologists entered this field, and also provides A RARE GLIMPSE OF THE EXCITEMENT AND PASSION THAT OCCURRED AT SOME OF THE MOST IMPORTANT AND DYNAMIC COMMUNITY TRAINING SETTINGS OVER THE PAST 40 YEARS."

Leonard A. Jason, PhD
Professor of Psychology and Director, Center for Community Research, DePaul University

More pre-publication
REVIEWS, COMMENTARIES, EVALUATIONS . . .

"THESE GRACEFULLY WRITTEN AND INTRIGUING ESSAYS are in many ways case studies of resilience among renowned academics who transcended notable obstacles in their personal lives and in their careers in pursuit of their deep interest in community psychology. For those of us who know the writers personally and for those who know of them only through their influential writing, these essays offer a fuller picture of each as a person worth knowing and admiring."

Murray Levine, JD, PhD
Distinguished Service Professor Emeritus
SUNY, Buffalo

Six Community Psychologists Tell Their Stories: History, Contexts, and Narrative

Six Community Psychologists Tell Their Stories: History, Contexts, and Narrative has been co-published simultaneously as *Journal of Prevention & Intervention in the Community*, Volume 28, Numbers 1/2 2004.

Dedication

To Lois and Jim Cook
and Colleen Loomis
whose competences, care
and timely intervention
made the completion
of this book possible

*Stories, finally, provide models
of the world–
another of those intuitive matters
we all know in our bones.*

No autobiography is completed, only ended.

–Jerome Bruner (2002)

Six Community Psychologists Tell Their Stories: History, Contexts, and Narrative

James G. Kelly, PhD
Anna V. Song, MA, BA
Editors

Six Community Psychologists Tell Their Stories: History, Contexts, and Narrative has been co-published simultaneously as *Journal of Prevention & Intervention in the Community*, Volume 28, Numbers 1/2 2004.

LONDON AND NEW YORK

Six Community Psychologists Tell Their Stories: History, Contexts, and Narrative has been co-published simultaneously as *Journal of Prevention & Intervention in the Community*, Volume 28, Numbers 1/2 2004.

First published 2004 by The Haworth Press, Inc.
Published 2013 by Routledge
2 Park Square, Milton Park, Abingdon, Oxon OX14 4RN
711 Third Avenue, New York, NY 10017, USA

Routledge is an imprint of the Taylor & Francis Group, an informa business

© 2004 by The Haworth Press, Inc. All rights reserved. No part of this work may be reproduced or utilized in any form or by any means, electronic or mechanical, including photocopying, microfilm and recording, or by any information storage and retrieval system, without permission in writing from the publisher.

Cover design by Kerry Mack

Library of Congress Cataloging-in-Publication Data

Six community psychologists tell their stories : history, contexts, and narrative / James G. Kelly, Anna V. Song, editors.
    p. cm.
   "Co-published simultaneously as Journal of prevention & intervention in the community, volume 28, numbers 1/2 2004."
   Includes bibliographical references and index.
   ISBN 978-0-789-02511-1 (pbk)
   1. Community psychologists–United States–Biography. 2. Community psychology–United States–History. 3. Community psychology–Vocational guidance. I. Kelly, James G. II. Song, Anna V.
RA790.55.S585 2004
362.2'092'2–dc22

2004010142

Six Community Psychologists Tell Their Stories: History, Contexts, and Narrative

CONTENTS

INTRODUCTION *James G. Kelly* *Anna V. Song*	1
On Becoming a Community Psychologist: The Intersection of Autobiography and History *Julian Rappaport*	15
An Accidental Community Psychologist *N. Dickon Reppucci*	41
Our Paradigms, Ourselves: Reflections on the Ecology of a Community Psychologist *Edison J. Trickett*	63
The Making of a Community Psychologist: Naïve Idealism, Supportive Contexts and Good Fortune *Jean Ann Linney*	81
Ecological Influences on an Ecologically-Oriented Community Psychologist *Marybeth Shinn*	103
Reflections on *Becoming* a Community Psychologist *Rhona S. Weinstein*	125
Memories *Henrika Kuklick*	149

COMMENTARY

Personal Destiny, Chance, and the Role of the Outsider
  in the Life Stories of Six Community Psychologists   153
    Dan P. McAdams

Index   159

ABOUT THE EDITORS

James G. Kelly, PhD, is Emeritus Professor, University of Illinois at Chicago and now Lecturer, Department of Psychology, University of California at Davis. Dr. Kelly was the first elected President of Division 27 of The American Psychological Association in 1968. In 1978 he received the award for distinguished contributions to Community Psychology and Community Mental Health from the Division. In 1997 he received the Senior Career Award for Distinguished Contributions to Psychology and the Public Interest from the American Psychological Association. In 2001 he received the Seymour Sarason Award from Division 27 and the Society for Community Research and Action. He is the co-author or co-editor of eight other books and over eighty publications. He has written on topics of the history of community psychology including a DVD with exemplars of the field.

Anna V. Song, MA, BA, is a doctoral candidate in personality and social psychology at the University of California, Davis. Her research interests include change and consistency in personality across domains, situations, social context, and time. This interest has led to work in political psychology, psychobiography, historiometry, at-a-distance methodologies, and the history of psychology. She is currently involved in research on cognitive decision-making factors that are characteristic to the person and variables that are impacted by environmental constraints. Her dissertation is a longitudinal, archival study of a cognitive-personality characteristic called integrative complexity to test whether it is a stable personality trait or a state-dependent construct.

INTRODUCTION

James G. Kelly
Anna V. Song

University of California at Davis

I have such admiration for people who can recount their lives in autobiography, because the connections are so complicated. I would never be able to straighten it out.

–John Cassavetes

These six stories present an opportunity to examine, at both the macro and micro levels, one of the fields of psychology–community psychology. These stories also provide examples to illustrate Thomas Kuhn's idea that "the tradition-shattering complements the tradition-bound activity of normal science" (Kuhn, 1962, p. 6). Each of the six

---

The editors are grateful that the following gave feedback on either early or later drafts and offered editorial and/or substantive comments and support: B. Eillen Altman, Dan Cervone, Alan C. Elms, Paul Dolinko, Jean Ann Linney, Wade Pickren, Thom Moore, Monisha Pasupathi, Julian Rappaport, Kate Isaacson, Dick Reppucci, Dan Romer, William Runyan, Carol Schneider, Beth Shinn, Lonnie Snowden, Ed Trickett, Rhona Weinstein, and Marc Alan Zimmerman.

contributors cites the issue of paradigmatic conflicts with clinical and/or social psychology, vintage 1960s and 1970s, as a catalyst for their involvement in community psychology. In addition, these stories provide qualitative data for thinking about the coherence of personality (Duncan & Agronick, 1995; Robins, Fraley, Roberts, & Trzesniewski, 2001; Roberts & DelVecchio, 2000; Caspi & Roberts, 1999). Several contributors explicitly question the notion that personality is "set like plaster" by age 30 (Costa & McCrae, 1994).These stories seem to fit a social-cognitive interpretation of personality: "Social cognitive approaches explore the psychological mechanisms that enable people to acquire social competences, adapt to the environment, plan and execute courses of action, and attain personal meaning in their lives. They address the reciprocal interactions between these personality structures and the socio-cultural environment" (Caprara & Cervone, 2000, p. 17).

ALTERNATIVE VIEWS OF AUTOBIOGRAPHY

There are contrasting points of view about the validity of autobiographical statements. The late mystery writer Eric Ambler sharply put forth a point of view in introducing his own autobiography. "Only an idiot believes that he can write the truth about himself" (Ambler, 1985, p. 18). Similarly, William Maxwell, the late *New Yorker* editor and novelist, maintained that every autobiography is a lie.

> What we refer to confidently as memory–meaning a moment, a scene, a fact that has been subjected to a fixative and therefore rescued from oblivion–is really a form of storytelling that goes on continually in the mind and often changes with the telling. Too many conflicting emotional interests are involved for life ever to be wholly acceptable and possibly it is the work of the storyteller to rearrange things so that they conform to this end. In any case, in talking about the past we lie with every breath we draw. (Maxwell, 1999, p. 27)

Ambler and Maxwell have made an important assertion. We all actively edit and construct a narrative of our lives that is definitely incomplete. The Editors argue that while the construction is incomplete, it is still informative and a first step in a dialogue with the story-teller about their lives.

In contrast, we have followed the leads of both Jerome Bruner and David Carr in affirming the value of autobiography. Bruner is pragmatic: "We cannot track people through life and observe or interrogate them each step of the way.... One viable alternative is obvious–to do the inquiry retrospectively, through autobiography ... I mean, simply, an account of what one thinks one did in what settings in what ways for what felt reasons" (Bruner, 1990, p. 119). And from Carr: "The narrator, in virtue of his/her retrospective view, picks out the most important events, traces the causal and motivational connections among them, and gives us an organized, coherent account" (Carr, 1986, p. 59). In other words, picking out events does not necessarily mean disguising events. Indeed, the editors argue that the selection or retrospective interpretation of past events is as interesting and substantive as an "accurate" portrayal of events. After reading the stories and talking with the six authors we agree with Dan McAdams' conjecture: "Life stories are based on autobiographical facts, but they go considerably beyond the facts as people selectively appropriate aspects of their experience and imaginatively construe both past and future to construct stories that make sense to them and their audiences, that vivify and integrate life and make it more meaningful" (McAdams, 2003, p. 187).

RESEARCH EVIDENCE ON AUTOBIOGRAPHICAL MEMORIES

There is an emerging literature on the nature, accuracy and meaning of autobiographies. The literature is useful in putting in context substantive issues when viewing these six stories (Fivush & Haden, 2003).

Pasupathi has reviewed the recent literature. She offered the idea that "audiences play a role in shaping recollections, and in doing so they also play a role in shaping identities" (Pasupathi, 2001, p. 663). Any story will be selective; what one chooses to present and what one chooses to withhold will be dependent on the audience. The audience for these stories is primarily the members of the Society for Community Research and Action, their family members, students, and, hopefully, future historians of psychology.

Constructing a coherent autobiographical statement of lives in progress raises epistemological issues. Kurt Back has reminded investigators that "these definitions ... do not come from a mathematical algorithm but depend on the biographer, the historical moment of the writing of the biography and the particular theory of the analysis. Here the definition and the importance of accuracy have changed. Accuracy is not necessarily equal to truth" (Back, 1994, p. 47). Robinson and Taylor (1998) concluded from their empirical research that "a narrative perspective is indispensable for understanding both autobiographical memory and self-narratives" (p. 141).

In presenting their accounts, each contributor recalls emotions that affected their views of themselves and their hopes for their careers, and note important occasions, both positive and negative, that were emotionally remembered. The role of emotions and emotional attachments is now being recognized as an appropriate topic for historians as well as psychologists (McLemee, 2003). Cognitive psychologists have focused attention on how emotions increase the accuracy and retrievability of memory (Bluck & Li, 2001). Contrary to Maxwell (1999), Bluck and Li believe emotions may lead not to distortion but to greater accuracy in recall. While studying emotions has been a major topic of research, the emotions of scientist/researcher have been neglected. In fact, most often the emotions of the researcher have been viewed as sources of error. It is only recently that the emotions of the investigator have been considered as not only salient but essential in the research process (Calhoun, 1989; Campbell, 2002).

Ochberg has observed that "culture circumscribes what we are able to talk about with each other" (Ochberg, 1988, p. 203). Certainly each of these contributors did withhold, on this occasion, painful, traumatic, or problematic events that may embarrass themselves or persons they know who are still living and who could be compromised if identified. This sensitivity is not lying. The late philosopher Bernard Williams has presented some hallmarks for a truthful assertion, which rest on a foundation of mutual respect and trust, and of honor and shame (Williams, 2002; McGinn, 2003). The editors are assuming these conditions applied here. These six stories constructed by the storytellers about themselves and their career development have currency as an affirmation of their own personal epistemologies and their unique ecologies. The reader may sense in taking in these stories that they express the "symbol systems" (to use Clifford Geertz's phrase), those interconnected concepts the authors use to communicate their stories (Geertz, 1984). When it all falls into place, the Editors are in agreement with Michael Lewis that "our belief about our current condition influences our current belief about the past, and our belief about the past in turn gives us meaning about the present" (Lewis, 2001, p. 75).

THE HISTORY OF PSYCHOLOGY AND THE HISTORY OF COMMUNITY PSYCHOLOGY

The history of psychology is gradually being appreciated as an attractive and informative subject in psychology (Pickren & Dewsbury, 2002). With few exceptions, the history of subfields and the social forces that affect the development of sub fields is still limited as a scholarly investigation. Donald A. Dewsbury has made a major start in examining the histories of the various Divisions of APA in five volumes (Dewsbury, 1996, 1997, 1999, 1999, 2001). In contrast, histories of research topics and constructs are often embedded in Annual Review Chapters or articles in the *Psychological Bulletin* or *Psychological Inquiry*.

Integrative reviews of the history of the field of community psychology have presented cogent observations about the contexts that have shaped the field (Revenson & Seidman, 2002). Textbooks in community psychology also include comments on the history and evolution of the field (Bloom, 1984; Dalton, Elias, & Wandersman, 2001; Duffy & Wong, 1996; Heller, Price, Reinharz, Riger, & Wandersman, 1986; Levine & Perkins,1987; Mann, 1978; Murrell, 1973; Rappaport, 1977; Rudkin, 2003). The history of community psychology is usually presented as interpretative accounts (Meritt, Greene, Jopp, & Kelly, 1999; Wilson, Hayes, Greene, Kelly, & Iscoe, 2003). The recent compilation of Robert Sternberg offers brief statements by sixteen psychologists who charted new directions (Sternberg, 2003). There are two collections of the autobiographies of sociologists (Berger, 1990; Glassner & Hertz, 2003). There are few first person accounts from community psychologists except for Seymour Sarason's (1988) autobiography.

For the whole field of psychology our model is the longstanding History of Psychology in Autobiography Series (Murchison, 1930, 1932, 1936; Boring, Langfeld, Werner, & Yerkes, 1952; Boring & Lindzey, 1967; Boring & Lindzey, 1973; Lindzey, 1980; Lindzey, 1989). This series bears out the statement of Gerda Lerner: "History is the archives of human experiences and of the thoughts of past generations; history is our collective memory" (Lerner, 1997, p. 52).

One attempt to document the field of community psychology is a DVD of Interviews with 17 early exemplars of the field. It presents the personal views of founders and refers to important events and social movements (Society for Community Research and Action, 2003). Some of the exemplars included in the DVD are: George Albee, Emory Cowen, Bill Fairweather, Jack Glidewell, Ira Iscoe, and Seymour Sarason. These accounts have pointed to the significance for community psychology of such topics as the effects of World War II on American society, the germinating events of the 1950s, the more visible expression of the civil rights movement in the 1960s, the community mental health movement, the second wave of feminism and the later significance of the resistance to the Vietnam War in the 1960s and 1970s.

THIS BOOK

This book which you are about to read builds upon the above historical foundations but does so in a different way. Since there has been some recognition and tribute given to the early contributors to the field in the DVD series noted above, the Editors chose to identify those persons whose careers in community psychology were just beginning at the time of the official founding of the field, 1965 and the next immediate era, the 1970s.

Taking as a baseline the series History of Psychology in Autobiography, the Editors asked six esteemed community psychologists to comment on the personal, situational and contextual factors that affected them and their careers. Invitations were extended to Julian Rappaport (PhD, University of Rochester, 1968), N. Dickon Reppucci (PhD, Harvard University, 1968) and Edison J. Trickett (PhD, Ohio State University, 1967).

A few years later, in the 1970s, there was more structure for the field, and there were more opportunities for women to pursue graduate careers in community psychology and to take part in the opportunities of this new field. Three esteemed women community psychologists were invited to report on the personal and contextual factors that impacted their choice of concentration in community psychology. They are: Jean Ann Linney (PhD, University of Illinois at Urbana, 1978), Beth Shinn (PhD, University of Michigan, 1978) and Rhona Weinstein (PhD, Yale University, 1973). The Editors believed that these six could elaborate the developmental and historical factors that affected their choices to become attracted to an emerging and as yet untested field.

These six persons were invited to take part not only as a result of their stature and esteem. They were also selected because they were students in six different doctoral programs. In addition to their own personal stories, some additional insights might be revealed about the various cultures of doctoral training in these different locations. Since these six persons have been elected as either Presidents and/or received prestigious awards by the APA Division of Community Psychology, they can be considered as eminent. For example, Rappaport's empirical research has been concerned with alternatives to professional care, particularly for those who are outside the mainstream of economic and social power. Substantive topics include juvenile justice, empowerment, self and mutual help, especially for people with a history of serious mental illness. Reppucci's contributions have been to provide an ecological perspective to the law as a framework for analyzing behavior. Trickett has applied an ecological perspective to community research and intervention, including the environmental assessment of high impact settings. Most recently he has been conducting research with refugee adolescents and their families and the settings they serve. Linney has worked on school desegregation and has evaluated social policy as a planned intervention. Most recently she has translated prevention methods for prevention practice. Shinn has studied the course and consequences of homelessness for families and single individuals, ways to end it, and to understand their relationships to individual well-being. Weinstein's research has focused on the culture of schooling and its impact on children's development. In particular she has focused on the dynamics of negative self-fulfilling prophecies, which are at the heart of unequal educational opportunity.

These three men and three women represent two "cohorts." As a group they also provide an opportunity to elicit insights about the gender differences and differential opportunities and constraints at different time periods: the 1960s and 1970s.

Each of the six was presented with suggested guidelines. The guidelines were stimulated by the first author's ecological perspective (Kelly, Ryan, Altman, & Stelzner, 2000) and research conducted as early as Lewis Terman's longitudinal study of giftedness and Simonton's work on scientific creativity (Terman, 1925; Simonton, 2000). Terman's and Simonton's combined work suggests that scientific leaders have developmental, personality and ecological similarities. The guidelines included: (a) PERSONAL (family background, including social status and family history, their parents' points of view about life and living, significant adults' influences, as well as identification of supportive people and events in their education); (b) CONTEXTUAL (social environmental, and cultural events, both national and local, affecting undergraduate, graduate and postgraduate experiences); and (c) INTELLECTUAL (the important ideas, people, and events that contributed to their identity formation as a community psychologist).

THE PROCESS

The six participants prepared a first draft and received feedback from the Editors. The feedback largely focused on asking for more elaboration of key points and events. The six chapters represented here are the stories of these community psychologists, about their development as community psychologists and how people, circumstances and events occurring at various times shaped their views about their academic identity. The statements seem to support Conway and Pleydell-Pearce's notions of reporting life time periods, general events, and specific events (Conway & Pleydell-Pearce, 2000). It must be said that these are not self-initiated statements but are in direct response to the Editors' request to prepare these autobiographies.

Themes

Social Marginality and Sex Discrimination. The significance of these stories is that the points of view and values of family members and those of significant teachers and faculty from elementary school through graduate school are defined and appreciated and on occasion noted as obstacles. Certainly issues of early experiences with family values and styles, class, ethnic status, racism, anti-Semitism and sense of power to obtain needed resources, are salient topics for the underlying motivation to choose to become a community psychologist. As Dean Simonton has proposed, the sense of marginality is present in the backgrounds of eminent psychologists. His assertion seems particularly apt for the lives of these six persons. As Simonton stated:

> There is a tendency for eminent personalities to come from homes that have experienced economic reversals or changes in fortune, even to the point of bankruptcy or impoverishment, but the type of adversity that has attracted the most scientific research is early parental loss or orphanhood. This literature has found a tendency for geniuses of all kinds to have experienced the death of one or both parents at an early age . . . the effects of parental loss seems verifiable enough to have inspired investigators to propose explanations for how such traumatic events might contribute to the development of genius. Three environmental hypotheses are perhaps most prominent. First, the trauma of parental loss produces a so-called bereavement syndrome, in which acts of achievement serve as emotional compensation. Second, such adverse events nurture the

development of a personality robust enough to overcome the many obstacles and frustrations standing in the path of achievement. Third, parental loss and other forms of extreme adversity may set a young talent along a developmental trajectory that diverges from the conventional. (Simonton, 1994, pp. 116-117)

The reader may find some basis for some or all of these explanations.

Most striking is the power of sex discrimination as a major constraint, particularly in the late 1960s and 1970s. Simonton has also commented on three features of cultural history that affect women pursuing professional careers. In addition to the differential socialization of boys and girls and the constraints of marriage and the family, he also states:

If the preceding two factors have not diverted an aspiring woman from her quest, active sex discrimination, may yet obstruct her path . . . Sometimes discrimination takes the form of subtle but prejudiced judgments: the assets of women may be undervalued in comparison to those of equally capable men. Other times the discrimination is blatant; Men who control the gateways to success often deliberately deny women access.... (Simonton, 1999, p. 219)

Once again, the reader will find many examples that are congruent with the Simonton thesis. These stories illustrate well how social norms can limit our choices. While such discriminatory experiences maybe more muted today, they are reminders that social and historical factors can be constraints at any time. Future historians of community psychology may focus on those seeming invisible factors that operate on all of us today!

Serendipity. In each of their stories, there are references to personal choices, chance events, coincidence, and serendipity; constructs of primary interest to the late Robert Merton, the distinguished sociologist, but not always noted in published discussions of personal histories. Albert Bandura has also pointed out the value of chance encounters (Bandura, 1982). But, it is more often poets, songwriters, and novelists who illustrate the significance of chance. Here is a statement, for example, by W. Somerset Maugham from one of his short stories "Virtue":

An incident of no moment, that might easily not have happened, has consequences that are incalculable. It looks as though blind chance ruled all things. Our smallest actions may affect profoundly the whole lives of people who have nothing to do with us. The story I have to tell would never have happened if one day I had not walked across the street. Life is really fantastic, and one has to have a peculiar sense of humour to see the fun of it. (Maugham, 1967, p. 1303)

Turning Points. In each of these stories the authors indicate that there were significant events, occasions or people who helped to generate a new or renewed sense of self. Often these are family members, teachers or others invested in them who sharpened their insights or pointed out new personal or career possibilities. The opportunity to be in new and foreign places, outside the U.S., also affected how they saw themselves and their situations. Negative experiences were also turning points as these events motivated them to do something else other than to tolerate their current plight; to chart a new direction for themselves. Sometimes turning points were sought after. Other times they happened unexpectedly.

Small Truths. It was interesting to us that sprinkled throughout the six stories there are affirmations about how the storytellers began to see their worlds. These affirmations we are labeling *Small Truths*. They often relate to their personal discoveries about themselves in response to their educational experiences. "What I did learn was that prediction based on test scores is fallible" or, "I have been extremely aware that my interpretation of reality, although informed by my training and experiences, is only one of many possible interpretations and not necessarily more accurate than other views" or, "These contrasting school settings and neighborhood peer groups became the arena to learn first hand about very different cultural, racial and socio-economic ways of being." There are others: "By the end of three semesters of graduate school I had lost interest in ever doing psychotherapy" and, "I also learned something about the weaknesses of quantitative analyses that fail to take contextual information into account" and, "I did not want to describe deficits, I wanted to fix them." These examples suggest that the autobiographical statement is a source of basic core beliefs about the authors and their professional identities.

The Power of Social Settings. There are other topics that are striking in these stories. One is the significance for the social settings at critical stages in their lives. For some it was libraries and playgrounds in grade school and high school. For others it was through music performance. For still others it was summer camp or other programmed summer activities. Later on in their graduate careers, opportunities to take part as a full member of a research program with faculty or specific educational environments like the Harvard Department of Social Relations, the Stanford Social Ecology Laboratory or the Yale Psycho-Educational

Clinic or taking part in international social causes, impacted their emerging professional and self identities. One contribution of these six stories is to argue once again for more understanding of the power and meaning of creating supportive social structures and social places that validate exploration, integration of ideas and self and professional identities.

To expand the discourse, two discussants were asked to add their observations. We are very pleased that Henrika Kuklick, a sociologist of science, and Dan McAdams, invested in narrative and personality, provided commentary.

The Editors hope that these essays will be helpful to historians of psychology, all community psychologists, and especially recent MAs and PhDs and new graduate students entering the field; helpful to them as they seek their personal goals and connect their personal aspirations to the field of community psychology. May these essays illuminate cultural constraints and enable obstacles to be addressed without the pain of feeling inadequate or limited or less competent. As Carr has suggested, "telling the story of my action or experience to others can organize or reorganize it for me; telling the story of my life can serve to make a sense of it that I have not been aware before" (Carr, 1986, p. 112). Future discussions might test this idea with these six storytellers! Historians of psychology may be interested as well in how these essays reflect the ways in which the larger cultural and social norms coupled with chance, coincidences and serendipity affect our careers and our lives.

REFERENCES

Ambler, E. (1985). *Here lies Eric Ambler: An autobiography.* New York: Farrar Straus Giroux.

Back, K.W. (1994). Accuracy, truth, and meaning in autobiographical reports. In N. Schwarz & S. Sudman (Eds.), *Autobiographical memory and the validity of retrospective reports* (pp. 39-53). New York: Springer-Verlag.

Bandura, A. (1982). The psychology of chance encounters and life paths. *American Psychologist, 37,* 747-755.

Berger, B. M. (Ed.) (1990). *Authors of their own lives.* Berkeley, CA: University of California Press.

Bloom, B. L. (1984). *Community mental health* (2nd ed.). Monterey, CA: Brooks/Cole.

Bluck, S., & Li, K.Z. (2001). Predicting memory completeness and accuracy: Emotion and exposure in repeated autobiographical recall. *Applied Cognitive Psychology, 15,* 145-158.

Boring, E.G., Langfeld, H. S., Werner, H., & Yerkes, R. M. (Eds.) (1952). *A history of psychology in autobiography* (Vol. 4). Worcester, MA: Clark University Press.
Boring, E. G., & Lindzey, G. (Eds.) (1967). *A history of psychology in autobiography* (Vol. 5). New York: Appleton-Century Crofts.
Boring, E. G., & Lindzey, G. (Eds.) (1973). *A history of psychology in autobiography* (Vol. 6). New York: Appleton Century Crofts.
Bruner, J. (1990). *Acts of meaning*. Cambridge, MA: Harvard University Press.
Bruner, J. (2002). *Making stories*. Cambridge, MA: Harvard University Press.
Calhoun, C. (1989) Subjectivity and emotion. *Philosophical Forum 20*, 195-210.
Campbell, R. C. (2002). *Emotionally involved: The impact of researching rape*. New York: Routledge.
Caprara, G. V., & Cervone, D. (2000). *Personality*. New York: Cambridge University Press.
Carr, D. (1986). *Time, narrative and history*. Bloomington, IN: Indiana University Press.
Caspi, A., & Roberts, B.W. (1999). Personality continuity and change across the life course. In L. A. Pervin & O. P. John (Eds.), *Handbook of personality: Theory and research (2nd ed.)* (pp. 300-326). New York: Guilford Press.
Conway, M. A., & Pleydell-Pearce, C. (2000). The construction of autobiographical memories in the self-memory system. *Psychological Review, 107*, 261-288.
Costa, P. T., Jr., & McCrae, R. R. (1994). Set like plaster? Evidence for the stability of adult personality. In T. F. Heatherton & J. L. Weinbergher (Eds.), *Can personality change?* (pp. 21-40). Washington, DC: American Psychological Association.
Dalton, J. H., Elias, M. J., & Wandersman, A. H. (2001). *Community psychology*. Belmont, CA: Wadsworth.
Dewsbury, D.A. (Ed.) (1996, 1997, 1999, 1999, 2001). *Unification through division* (Vols.1-5). Washington, DC: American Psychological Association.
Duffy, K. G., & Wong, F. Y. (1996). *Community psychology*. Boston: Allyn & Bacon.
Duncan, L. E., & Agronick, G. S. (1995). The intersection of life stage and social events: Personality and life outcomes. *Journal of Personality and Social Psychology, 69*, 558-568.
Fivush, R., & Haden, C. (2003). *Autobiographical memory and the construction of the narrative self*. Mahwah, NJ: Lawrence Erlbaum.
Geertz, C. (1984). Anti-anti relativism. *American Anthropologist, 86*, 263-278.
Glassner, B., & Hertz, R. (2003). *Our studies, ourselves: Sociologists' lives and work*. New York: Oxford University Press.
Heller, K., Price, R. H., Reinharz, S., Riger, S., & Wandersman, A. H. (1984). *Psychology and community change* (2nd ed.). Pacific Grove, CA: Brooks/Cole.
Kelly, J.G., Ryan, A. M., Altman, B. E., & Stelzner, S. P. (2000). Understanding and changing social systems: An ecological view. In J. Rappaport & E. Seidman (Eds.), *Handbook of community psychology* (pp. 133-159). New York: Kluwer Academic/Plenum.
Kuhn, T. S. (1962). *The structure of scientific revolutions*. Chicago: University of Chicago Press.
Lerner, G. (1997). *Why history matters*. New York: Oxford University Press.
Levine, M., & Perkins, D. V. (1987). *Principles of community psychology*. New York: Oxford University Press.

Lewis, M. (2001). Issues in the study of personality development. *Psychological Inquiry, 12*, 67-85.
Lindzey, G. (Ed.) (1980). *A history of psychology in autobiography* (Vol. 7). San Francisco: W.H. Freeman.
Lindzey, G. (Ed.) (1989). *A history of psychology in autobiography* (Vol. 8). Stanford, CA: Stanford University Press.
Mann, P.A. (1978). *Community psychology.* New York: Free Press.
Maugham, W. S. (1967). *The complete short stories: IV. The human element and other stories.* New York: Washington Square Press, Inc.
Maxwell, W. (1980/1997). *So long, see you tomorrow.* New York: Harvill.
McAdams, D. (2003). Identity and life stories. In R. Fivush & C. A. Haden (Eds.), *Autobiographical memory and the construction of a narrative self* (pp. 197-223). Mahwah, NJ: Lawrence Erlbaum Associates.
McGinn, C. (2003). Isn't it the truth? *New York Review of Books, L(6)*, 70-73.
McLemee, S. (2003). Getting emotional. *Chronicle of Higher Education, L(4)*, A14-16.
Meritt, D. M., Greene, G. F., Jopp, D. A., & Kelly, J. G. (1999). A history of division 27 (Society for community research and action). In D. A. Dewsbury (Ed.), *Unification through division: Histories of the divisions of the American Psychological Association* (Vol. 111) (pp. 73-99). Washington, DC: American Psychological Association.
Murchison, C. (Ed.) (1930). *A history of psychology in autobiography* (Vol. 1). Worcester, MA: Clark University Press.
Murchison, C. (Ed.) (1932). *A history of psychology in autobiography* (Vol. 2). Worcester, MA: Clark University Press.
Murchison, C. (Ed.) (1936). *A history of psychology in autobiography* (Vol. 3). Worcester, MA: Clark University Press.
Murrell, S. A. (1973). *Community psychology and social systems.* New York: Behavioral Publications.
Ochberg, R. L. (1988). Life stories and the psychosocial construction of careers. In D. R. McAdams & R. L. Ochberg (Eds.), *Psychobiography and life narratives* (pp. 173-204). Durham, NC: Duke University Press.
Pasupathi, M. (2001). The social construction for the personal past and its implications for adult development. *Psychological Bulletin, 127*, 651-672.
Pickren, W., & Dewsbury, D. A. (Eds.) (2002). *Evolving perspectives on the history of psychology.* Washington, DC: American Psychological Association.
Rappaport, J. (1977). *Community psychology.* New York: Holt, Rinehart & Winston.
Revenson, T. A., & Seidman, E. (2002). Looking backward and moving forward: Reflections on a quarter century of community psychology. In T.A. Revenson (Ed.), *A quarter century of community psychology* (pp. 3-31). New York: Kluwer.
Roberts, B. W., & DelVecchio, W. F. (2000). The rank-order consistency of personality traits from childhood to old age: A quantitative review of longitudinal studies. *Psychological Bulletin, 126*, 3-25.
Robins, R. W., Fraley, R.C., Roberts, B., & Trzesniewski, K. H. (2001). A longitudinal study of personality in young adulthood. *Journal of Personality, 69*, 617-640.
Robinson, J. A., & Taylor, L. R. (1998). Autobiographical memory and self-narratives: A tale of two stories. In C. R. Thompson, D. J. Herrmann, D. Bruce, J. D. Reed, D.G.

Payne, & M. P. Toglia (Eds.), *Autobiographical memory* (pp. 125-143). Mahwah, NJ: Lawrence Erlbaum.

Rudkin, J. K. (2003). *Community psychology*. Upper Saddle River, NJ: Prentice Hall.

Sarason, S.B. (1988). *The making of an American psychologist*. San Francisco: Jossey Bass.

Simonton, D. K. (1994). *Greatness: Who makes history and why*. New York: Guilford Press.

Simonton, D. K. (1999). Talent and its development: An emergenic and epigenetic model. *Psychological Review, 106*, 435-457.

Simonton, D. K. (2002). *Great psychologists and their times: Scientific insights into psychology's history*. Washington, DC: American Psychological Association.

Society for Community Research & Action (2003). *Exemplars of community psychology* [DVD]. Edmond, OK: Author.

Sternberg, R. J. (2003). *Psychologists defying the crowd*. Washington, DC: American Psychological Association.

Terman, L. M. (1925). *Mental and physical traits of a thousand gifted children*. Stanford, CA: Stanford University Press.

Williams, B. (2002). *Truth and truthfulness*. Princeton, NJ: Princeton University Press.

Wilson, B. M., Hayes, E., Greene, G. J., Kelly, J. G., & Iscoe, I. (2003) Community psychology. In D.F. Freedheim (Ed.), *History of psychology (Vol. 1)* of I. B. Weiner (Ed.), *Handbook of psychology* (pp. 431-449). New York: John Wiley & Sons.

On Becoming a Community Psychologist: The Intersection of Autobiography and History

Julian Rappaport

University of Illinois at Urbana-Champaign

SUMMARY. Recounts the author's professional life history in the context of his personal life story. Reflects on the ways in which history and autobiography combine to create life pathways that are experienced as individually chosen, yet historically determined. Recounts the author's family life, neighborhood experiences, early education in the Philadelphia public schools, and the impact of post-World War II government programs including the GI Bill and the establishment of United States Public Health Service fellowships. Considers the influence of African American writers and the civil rights movement, as well as women returning to school, the culture of medical schools and the influence of mentors in the formation of a professional identity. Recounts the discovery of the community mental health movement and the search for a social justice agenda that led to Community Psychology. Ultimately, the author views himself as an "insider/outsider," whose personal and professional identity crosses traditional boundaries and welcomes paradoxical, narrative and qualita-

---

Address correspondence to: University of Illinois at Urbana-Champaign, Department of Psychology, 603 E. Daniel Street, Champaign, IL 61820.

[Haworth co-indexing entry note]: "On Becoming a Community Psychologist: The Intersection of Autobiography and History." Rappaport, Julian. Co-published simultaneously in *Journal of Prevention & Intervention in the Community* (The Haworth Press, Inc.) Vol. 28, No. 1/2, 2004, pp. 15-39; and: *Six Community Psychologists Tell Their Stories: History, Contexts, and Narrative* (eds: James G. Kelly, and Anna V. Song) The Haworth Press, Inc., 2004, pp. 15-39. Single or multiple copies of this article are available for a fee from The Haworth Document Delivery Service [1-800-HAWORTH, 9:00 a.m. - 5:00 p.m. (EST). E-mail address: docdelivery@haworthpress.com].

http://www.haworthpress.com/web/JPIC
© 2004 by The Haworth Press, Inc. All rights reserved.
Digital Object Identifier: 10.1300/J005v28n01_02

tive approaches to research and practice. *[Article copies available for a fee from The Haworth Document Delivery Service: 1-800-HAWORTH. E-mail address: <docdelivery@haworthpress.com> Website: <http://www.HaworthPress.com> © 2004 by The Haworth Press, Inc. All rights reserved.]*

KEYWORDS. Life history, social history, professional development, public policy, community mental health, Community Psychology

The intersection of autobiography and history is something I have always taken for granted. My earliest memories include a father in uniform who returned from war to die from what was called "a service connected disability." I never doubted that life would be lived in the context of a larger world, not an abstract larger world, but one that is concrete, one that enters the door unbidden and takes me by the hand or by the heart to places unexpected.

FAMILY LIFE (1942-1948)

I was five years old when my father, Louis Joseph Rappaport, died, leaving my mother to care for me and my thirteen month old sister, Joan. I knew he did not intend to die, so it must have had something to do with the world. When my mother (who was named Fanny, but always called herself Fay) married Ben, a man she neither loved nor admired, it was because she could not conceive of going to work, leaving her children in the care of others, or being without a man. These were not ideas she invented. They are a perfect reflection of the culture in which she lived–a child of first generation immigrants, working class, Jewish, in post World War II America–where women returned home from the factories of the war effort to make room for returning veterans. Fay had not worked outside her home during the war and she would not do it now. Of course, the way she arrived at this decision was also determined by who she was, by her unique personality.

I never doubted that in the intersection of autobiography and history, personality, and will, play important roles. My mother was offered a job in the post office, where my father had worked before going off to England to fight a European fascism and anti-Semitism that were not all that different from what my grandparents had sought to escape when they left Europe almost half a century earlier. I knew that other women worked, and that the step-father who was now present as a constant angry and inadequate figure, a failed salesman and source of daily anxiety in my life, was not an inevitable family member. But there he was. The daily arguments, the constant ways in which both of these adults insulted each other, my awareness of his resentment of me as not his son, but as a reminder of a fallen hero who he could never replace, made life at home something to be avoided.[1] Mostly I avoided home by going to playgrounds (first to play children's games and later to play on well lit, outdoor basketball courts, almost every night of the week) and libraries. Playgrounds and libraries were places where I could lose myself in other worlds. I have always loved both settings. I have always been thankful for the sense of community that provokes civic leaders and citizens to support them. My love of libraries is founded in the family story that my father had loved books, and had owned a large library that was destroyed by fire while in storage during the war. I have never been able to verify the story, nor do I have any of his books or recall ever being read to as a child. But I do have fond memories of fighting with my sister over who would be first to read the "funnies" in our daily newspaper, *The Philadelphia Bulletin.*

EARLY (MIS)EDUCATION (1948-1960)

My father died in February of 1948, three months after my fifth birthday. Before the year was out, my mother was remarried. Ben did not adopt us, and Joan and I retained our father's name, a circumstance I did not understand but came to like very much. I felt a keen sense of uniqueness from my name. Throughout my education in the Philadelphia public schools I never met another person with my first name. In those days, at least in my neighborhood, most children had the same last name as their parents. Every year in school I had to endure the same interrogation from a new teacher: "Why is your mother's name different from yours?" Eventually I learned that saying my father had died in the war, that my mother had remarried, and that my step-father had not adopted me, invoked a sympathetic response, and I learned not to mind the curiosity.

My mother had dropped out of school after the 10th grade; but my father was a graduate of Central High School, the all boys public school in Philadelphia that everyone considered to be for smart kids and intellectuals. Today I wear his plain gold high school graduation ring. The inscription, "30," marking his year of graduation, is barely visible. It was at that school that my Uncle John (who married my mother's older sister) taught history, and that his son, two years older than me (who would go on to become a mathematics professor) was a star student. I was expected to attend that school too, and I did for one year. As a freshman I wanted to play football, which I did, while failing every subject. I attended summer school so as not to be "left back," and transferred to the local high school in time to join the football team. I had enough sense to manage to get by as a "B" student in a considerably less demanding environment, much to the dismay of my uncle and cousin. Northeast, the high school I attended for the next three years, is the one that, several years after I left, was captured in Frederick Wiseman's classic documentary, "High School." Many of the same teachers were still there, including my football coach and my counselor.

My counselor advised me that, given my SAT scores, I was not likely to graduate from college. She suggested alternative career plans, a suggestion I learned only years later, watching the Wiseman documentary, that she seemed to enjoy making to others as well. But I never took her advice seriously. What I did learn was that prediction based on test scores is fallible. I always knew I would go to college. I had learned from my mother's stories that this had been something my "real" father had desired for himself, and I also learned that I was destined to be "like him." Although I have very few memories of my father, for most of my life he has existed as an ideal figure to be emulated. When I was thirty-five years old I dedicated the textbook, "Community Psychology: Values Research and Action," to him. I wrote that he would "enjoy knowing that his memory rests on library shelves." I still believe that.

What I learned growing up in our row house, where every word we said too loud could be heard by our neighbor, was how to negotiate the politics of a chaotic family life. This turned out to be a good training ground for clinical work, and for negotiating the politics of organizations and communities. By the time I was twelve I was regularly serving as a kind of diplomatic envoy between warring nations, one male and one female. When I awoke each morning, if Fay and Ben were yelling obscenities at each other I knew the world was in predictable order. If I awoke to silence, I was startled. Years later, my sister and I remembered independently thinking that when we heard our mother and Ben talking at night, as we lay in our beds, we assumed they were planning what tomorrow's arguments would be. Each of us had tried to put some rationality into an irrational family life. We both recall being surprised to discover that some of our friends had normal conversations with their parents. Although he never hit me I was always fearful of Ben. We never spent a comfortable moment together. He was always threatening to leave, and this seemed to scare my mother. On more than one occasion, fearful for my mother, I found myself begging him to stay when I really wished he would leave. I am certain that what later became called "clinical skills" were acquired in the heat of growing up, rather than in the textbooks or practica of graduate school. Perhaps this is why, from the very beginning of my career, I was interested in the ways in which ordinary people, called by psychologists "nonprofessionals," or lately, "mentors," or members of mutual help organizations, care for one another without professional assistance.

PAYING FOR COLLEGE (1960-1964)

My mother, despite her own lack of education, and even in the absence of books in our home or pictures on our walls, communicated to me the expectation that I would go to college. Although we had very little money, paying for college was one of the few things for which money was not a concern. History, on this occasion, was my friend. The era in which my sister and I grew up, post World War II America, has been laughed at for its "father knows best" illusions, its "little boxes on the hill side," and its cultural and social dullness. But not enough attention has been paid to this era's use of government policy as a means to help ordinary citizens. Because of what came to be known as the GI Bill, many veterans returning from the war were given an opportunity to go to college, paid for by the U.S. Government. This legislation supporting veterans benefits was renewed in the 1950's. As the surviving children of a deceased war veteran my sister and I were eligible to receive his GI Bill benefits. We were each allotted $110 per month for 9 months a year, for four years, to use for college expenses. We also obtained $400 per year scholarships from a veterans service organization. This was more than sufficient to pay for our college books and tuition at the state supported institutions we both attended (Penn State and Temple), and enabled me to use the money I earned working twenty hours a week as a grocery clerk (I kept the dog food and soda aisles stocked) for my other living expenses during the five years between my senior year in high school and the start of graduate school.

Once in graduate school I continued on the government dole as a United States Public Health Service (USPHS) Fellow, yet another program the U.S. Congress had created to help its citizens. This one was designed to train mental health professionals to handle the demand of so many returning servicemen. I am, to this day, amazed that in addition to paying the costs of graduate school, the government actually gave me a stipend ($150 per month) to live on while I was getting an education. This government policy, along with a similar program administered by the Veterans Administration, induced psychology departments all over the United States to open up their ivory towers to develop clinical, and ultimately community oriented, education. History and autobiography had conspired to shape my future.

THE NEIGHBORHOOD (1942-1946)

Until I was three, my mother lived with my father's family in north Philadelphia, or in a small apartment in an area known as Strawberry Mansion. "The Mansion," as they referred to it, was populated mostly by eastern European Jewish immigrants whose children would later move to newer areas (financed largely by low cost government loans to veterans) on the edges of the city, just as this deteriorating neighborhood was inherited by Black families. My father's father worked in a popular bath house and earned a decent living compared to my mother's father, Julius, for whom I am named. Julius was a window washer who died before I was born. I recall going with my paternal grandmother to Shull (synagogue). She was an Orthodox Jew who spoke only Yiddish and lived with her unmarried daughter in the same rented house until her death. In Shull we sat with the women and children in the balcony (much to my delight) while the men prayed separately below us. I liked going with her and watching the bearded men, in a sea of prayer shawls, nodding below.

PUBLIC HOUSING (1947-1952)

When my father returned to the United States, before he died, we moved into a public housing project in southwest Philadelphia, a decidedly non-Jewish environment. Here for the first time I encountered people with guns who hung the deer they had shot outside their windows to keep them refrigerated. Living in public housing was an early clue to the power of government policy to provide for its citizens, since we could find no other affordable housing. This experience also remains as a memory of bureaucratic authority. My mother constantly worried that she would be discovered to have a prohibited washing machine in our apartment; and there were only limited ways in which the decor could be personalized. Bartram Village was built on the former estate of one of Philadelphia's elite historical figures, John Bartram, who had created beautiful gardens and planted trees that I learned to climb. But the apartment building itself had concrete floors, steel doors and walls painted in a particular shade of green that I recognized when I first encountered the inside of a state mental hospital. I lived in Bartram Village until I was nine years old. Although at that time there were no African Americans living in this project, my father had worked with African Americans at the post office and had at least one friend who for many years was the only Black person I knew. But my mother tended to favor progressive politics and held the Roosevelts and Adali Stevenson in great esteem. I knew that my grandfather had been a supporter of Norman Thomas, although I did not know who he was. I assume that somehow these political leanings got into our family sensibilities. My sister, Joan, has had a life long career as a social activist. She has been a community organizer, the Executive Director of the Illinois branch of the National Abortion Rights League, and the director of a program for the prevention of domestic violence. Her husband, Peter, is a labor union organizer.

THE NEW NEIGHBORHOOD (1952-1960)

Our move to a working class, Jewish neighborhood of row houses in the new northeast part of the city gave me a sudden sense of belonging. I was in the fourth grade and had until then encountered an uncomfortable but impossible to describe lack of fit between my sensibilities and those of my peers and teachers. I was physically small, and I recall feeling like an outsider listening in on school. I remember being in second grade "remedial reading," and also being asked to see the school counselor who wanted to know why I fidgeted so much in class. I have a very clear memory of this conversation, and in my mind's eye I can see the counselor's knee, revealed just outside her skirt, staring at me. I told her I was bored.

The new elementary school I attended was named for S. Solis Cohen, a well known Jewish physician. My first teacher was named Mrs. Shapiro, and suddenly everyone sounded like me. All this was of course unremarked upon, but I recall feeling more comfortable in school. It turned out that most of the teachers were not Jewish, although the students were; but we did not mind the daily Bible readings that were then a part of every morning for all Pennsylvania public school students. I did not even mind it when, after being elected class president, my sixth grade teacher had me impeached for being a behavior problem. I enjoyed what seemed to me to be prominence among my peers and had no sense that it was different to be notorious than admired. My recollection of the reason for my impeachment is hazy, but I think it had to do with too much clowning around when I was supposed to be chairing class meetings.

I continued to be a happy but non-serious student through junior high school, when I suddenly grew to my present height, before I was sent across town to the serious high school I would fail out of. But while I was there, unbeknownst to anyone, including me, I had been influenced by several teachers. I wish I could recall the name of the teacher who told us about literary magazines like the *Saturday Review* that I found in the library and subscribed to as soon as I started to work and had money of my own. There I encountered the likes of Norman Cousins, its long time editor, and others who had little to do with school work but a lot to do with educating me.

When I was a high school student, in the last years of the 1950s, Martin Luther King Jr. appeared on the cover of *Time*, and the civil rights movement was entering the consciousness of the nation. In the white suburb of northeast Philadelphia I do not recall much interest. In my senior year I had decided to write a research paper on "The Negro in American Literature." I could find no materials in my school or local branch library. For reasons I do not remember, rather than going to the main branch of the Philadelphia Public Library, I found my way to a small center city library run by the NAACP. It was here, under the guidance of a gentle African American woman librarian, that I encountered writers (I especially recall reading Richard Wright) I had no idea existed, and who fostered in me a sense of justice for which I as yet had no outlet.

GOING TO COLLEGE (1960-1964)

Despite my mediocre school record I managed to get admitted to a branch campus of Penn State located just outside of Philadelphia, expecting to become a history teacher. In those days the Ogontz Campus, located on the grounds of a former private girls school (it even had a duck pond) was a two year institution and people were expected to transfer to the main campus after their sophomore year. With only 900 students, and faculty who were teachers rather than researchers, it was an ideal setting for me. It was here that my friendship with Edward Seidman, who had been a teammate on my high school football team, blossomed. Ed was always a lot more organized than me, and he had begun to create, the term before I arrived on campus, an Intramural Board to foster campus athletics and other forms of competition and comradrie. He invited me to join with him and together we developed an organization that had most of the campus involved in some form of competition ranging from football leagues to chess matches. Some of these associations led us into campus politics and writing letters to the campus newspaper. Thus was I introduced to community organization and participation as a vehicle for social and political engagement. I had no idea that this experience would be followed years later by a long term collaboration with Ed in our professional lives.

Although I was sure I would flunk out, being a college student energized me. I only had to attend each class three times a week, nobody took attendance, looked at my notebooks, or monitored my behavior! I could not believe it; this was easier than high school, and indeed I did much better. For the first time school seemed like fun. The teachers at Ogontz inspired me. My English teacher, Mr. Bilder, was a young, bald, gay, man who told me I could write. He introduced me to the beat writers. I loved Allen Ginsberg and Lawrence Ferlinghetti, who seemed to be able to make ordinary experiences ("the dog trots freely in the street") into poetry. I took the introductory psychology course with an instructor who taught from a wheelchair. We read Hilgard's second edition. His lectures seemed to be a recitation of all the things that seemed most obvious to me. I wondered how I already knew about them, but that did not make me any less anxious about tests, and I developed a habit of rewriting my notes and reciting them aloud. The most influential instructor I had was an experimental psychologist, Dr. Jean Smith. She helped me to understand the meaning of a "significant difference," and she was one in my life. Almost twenty-five years later Ed Seidman and I, who had taken the same classes with her, dedicated a book, "Reframing Social Issues," to Jean Smith.

MY FIRST MENTOR, MARRIAGE AND GRADUATE SCHOOL

It was Jean Smith who said to me, "So, you should start thinking about graduate school." I had no idea that people went to school after college, other than to be doctors or lawyers. She wanted me to apply to her alma mater, Duke, in experimental psychology, but I had become interested in clinical psychology, in part because she introduced me to it. Since Ogontz was a small school even the experimentalists who taught us how the eye functions in perception introduced us to psychologists in practice. Dr. Smith arranged a visit for our class to a nearby residential treatment center for emotionally disturbed children. I was introduced to a young psychologist who had not yet gone to Yale to create the Psycho-Educational Clinic with Seymour Sarason, Ira Goldenberg, and others who would later influence me. I still think of Murray Levine as the first "real psychologist" I ever met. This is the only time I spoke to him until many years later, when I met him again as a colleague; but for some reason I always remembered meeting him. I can still see Dr. Levine in my mind's eye, talking seriously with our small group of undergraduates from the two year campus nearby. When I later discovered that he wrote about things I cared about I was once again astounded by my good fortune.

After two years at Ogontz, and one term at the main campus of Penn State, I completed my undergraduate education at Temple University so that I could live and work in Philadelphia. By transferring to Temple I was able to keep my (union scale salary) job at the supermarket. At both universities I took personally influential courses in philosophy and comparative religion. I married my high school sweetheart, Arlene Goldstein, in January of my senior year. Although she was an artist she took a job as a hairdresser while I went to school and worked at the grocery store. I met several older (than me) women who were going to school now that their children were not so dependent on them. They were usually the brightest people in class. I had never had adult women in my classes before. They wanted to talk seriously about the things we were learning and I used to like to study for tests with them because they were very serious about doing well in school, yet seemed entirely non-competitive about it. It would be twenty years before Arlene would do the same thing.

Arlene had grown up with two sisters, one of whom was very seriously physically disabled by cerebral palsy. Arlene's mother cared for her at home (she could not speak and had to be fed) until her death at the age of thirty-six. As a teenager, when I first met Arlene, she was often involved in the care of her sister. Beverly, who suffered from frequent grand mal seizures, was often placed, in her wheelchair, in the center of the household, and reactions to her by visitors served as one test Arlene's mother used to see if Arlene's friends were worthy of her time. I used to love to talk to Arlene's mother, late at night after Arlene had gone to bed. Arlene grew up in a loving family in which she was expected to learn all the domestic duties of women, but not, even though it was already obvious that she had artistic skills, to go to school. Indeed, her mother often kept her home from school to help with Beverly.

When our youngest daughter, Amy, was nine years old (1981) Arlene went to college for the first time. After graduation she became the art teacher at a residential school for neglected, abused and emotionally disturbed children. But now it was 1964, and the previous November, searching for my car parked on a narrow north Philadelphia street near Temple's campus, I had learned of the assassination of John F. Kennedy from an older Black man sitting on the broken stoop in front of his apartment. When Lyndon Johnson became President world events again changed my life. His policy of "a war on poverty" would soon provide a concrete channel for my growing passion about social justice. But I did not know that yet. For now I wanted to be a psychotherapist.

I applied to graduate schools without much knowledge of one department as opposed to another. I did not get in to Duke, but I had already been accepted at Purdue, where I was told I would be a VA trainee, when I got a call from the University of Rochester, where I had earlier been designated as an "alternate." I decided to accept the offer at Rochester because I thought of it as small and private, something different than the public schools I had attended up until then. I had no idea that my interest in psychology was about to be redirected. Currently, I am dismayed that most psychology departments seem to expect applicants to graduate school to know exactly what narrow part of the field (and with whom) they want to spend the rest of their life studying, before they are admitted. When I started graduate school I had no idea what kind of research I wanted to do.

GRADUATE EDUCATION (1964-1968)

On a late summer day in 1964 Arlene and I drove into Rochester, New York. Our blue Volkswagen Beetle pulled a small rented trailer that held our most important possessions: clothes, a hi-fi stereo, books, and the bricks and boards on which they would be stacked. The first thing we saw, as we pulled off the freeway, were military vehicles and the National Guard in combat gear. There had been a riot on the streets of Rochester's Black community that summer. The smugness of an Eastman Kodak and Xerox Corporation dominated town had been shattered. It would soon be a time when organizers like Saul Alinsky would be invited to the community. But the River Campus of the University of Rochester existed as an almost separate world. The small, insular campus was quiet, and I immediately became engaged in the work of a first year graduate student who wanted to be a clinical psychologist. I had the vague idea that I would like to "help people." Arlene got a job as a hairdresser, and I had the USPHS fellowship that enabled me to spend all my time in class or the library, compliments of Uncle Sam.

The first year program at Rochester, in addition to courses in research methods (which, oddly, I thought, devoted a lot of time to how to build electronic circuits for the construction of experimental devices), and statistics, was built around "Pro Seminar." All graduate students were required to take a series of four to six week courses with faculty from every area of the department, unless you were "exempted" by taking an exam. I had spent my summer doing in-take interviews at a public mental hospital, reading E. G. Boring's "History of Experimental Psychology," and a variety of books on clinical and abnormal psychology, so I managed to skip those sections of Pro Seminar and take a course in Advanced Abnormal Psychology with Melvin Zax. Here I read Otto Fenichel's classic text on the "Psychoanalytic Theory of Neurosis," and the "Collected Works of Harry Stack Sullivan," compiled by his students. I laughed at Fenichel and loved Sullivan. I still do. But Pro Seminar was the eye opener for me. In addition to learning some basic neurology, social and developmental psychology, I was introduced to the study of perception by Professor Ralph Haber. Beyond the subject matter, Haber himself captured my attention. He was the first person who asked me, frequently, "what are the implications" of some data or fact I offered. Later I would be similarly struck by John Flavell who had just published his text on Piaget and from whom I took a course in developmental psychology.

First year clinical students (seven males and one female) took courses from two young assistant professors: Ralph Barocas taught us the thinking of people like Lee Chronbach and Paul Meehl, Tex Garner, Harry Hake and Charles Eriksen, Donald Campbell and Donald Fiske, Doug Jackson and Samuel Messick on test construction. Jay Efran, a Julian Rotter student, introduced us to an early version of social learning theory. Thus was I prepared as a skeptic to begin my second year in which I would combine class work in clinical psychology (testing, therapy) with practice, three days a week on the psychiatric unit of a general hospital, The University of Rochester's Strong Memorial Hospital. Before I started at the hospital I spent the summer reading novels that had been recommended by friends who seemed to be much better educated than me. Howard Kahn, a student in the experimental program who later became a clinician, gave me a long list of books, and so did Ralph Barocas, our first year professor who I got to know more as a person than as a teacher. Among the many authors I read that summer were Dostoevsky, Faulkner, Huxley, Mailer, Hemingway, Ellison, Virginia Woolf and

Thomas Hardy. I also read Claude Brown's powerful autobiography about growing up as a Black man in America, "Manchild in the Promised Land." There were quite a few others, but I especially recall being struck by Hemingway's short sentences. These novels influenced me as much as the official curriculum. I learned more about how to write from reading them than from reading journals. I had wonderful peers during my four years at Rochester, among them future community psychologists Jack Chinsky, Ramsay Liem and Tom Wolff. Irwin Sandler joined the program the year before I left. Tom, who at that time seemed to be more interested in developmental psychology, was always a student leader, and one can see in retrospect his skills as an action oriented organizer who has the ability to conceptualize what he is doing.

THE MEDICAL SCHOOL

My year at the medical school hospital was formative. I wore a white coat. I gave and interpreted projective tests under the wise counsel of Bertram Stöffelmayr, a young psychologist from Vienna, who had recently completed a post doctoral appointment in England with H. J. Eysenck. I was supervised by a very skilled and practical psychologist named Floyd Wylie, the only African American on the psychology staff, as I worked with a patient in rehabilitation following an automobile accident. I shared an office with a brilliant and charming advanced graduate student, an African American woman named Janice Porter, who was very kind to me. She was much better educated than me, and had an intellectually sophisticated understanding of herself and the world. She gently taught me, with little formality, the ways a professional behaves, even when he feels like a working class kid, out of place among professionals. However, I learned that I could not spend my life doing psychological testing and psychotherapy, and certain experiences stand out in my memory of that year as a psychology trainee in a medical school.

Stöffelmayr and I did a psychological assessment of a woman who, as we wrote in our report, was at high risk for suicide, and perhaps a danger to her children. She stayed her thirty days covered by insurance, was released to the State Hospital when her insurance ran out, then sent home where she killed her two children before unsuccessfully trying to kill herself. This was the first time I realized that economics and hospital policies and procedures had more to do with the care of people than anything I had learned in school. But this event was only the most dramatic of the pattern I saw.

I learned that people who came into the psychiatric unit were often interesting objects of study for grand rounds, but just as often in need of assistance that the mental health community could rarely provide. I learned that the way they were treated often had very little to do with their diagnosis, although we spent an inordinate amount of time trying to categorize them. The experience of grand rounds was instructive, both as social ritual and as a window that revealed the hospital's hierarchical organization.. The room where a patient would be presented for an interview had a long table where at one end the Professor, a senior psychiatrist, interviewed the patient of the day, often a woman in hospital night clothes and robe, who sat stared at by men in suits, smoking pipes. Nearby sat other psychiatrists in ankle length white coats, further down the table were the residents, in mid-thigh coats, and then medical students who looked like bus boys in their short white coats. Psychologists and nurses sat away from the table, except for the few who were most senior. I recall wishing I had a stethoscope to leave dangling from my pocket when I went to the coffee shop to mingle among the people.

MY SECOND MENTOR

A turning point in my graduate education came when I decided that I could not return to the medical school setting. As I entered my third year of graduate school (1966-1967) I decided to ask Emory L. Cowen if he would let me be a research assistant for him. I barely knew him at the time, but his reputation was as the most demanding faculty member in the department. During our required second year research presentations (Professor Barocas had supervised my experimental study in which I tested the frustration-aggression hypothesis by giving mild electric shock to unsuspecting undergraduates) Cowen was the person who everyone knew would ask the most impossible to answer questions. My psychoanalytic training led me to understand that asking to work for him was "counter-phobic." Since my step-father entered my life I had learned to question authority and to work at my best when I was free to do things my own way. Now I was approaching the person with the most authority in the program. I do not think this request was content based, because I knew very little about the "Primary Mental Health Project" that Cowen had started in the public schools. I am sure I was partly motivated by wanting to avoid going back to the hospital setting, and I suspect I was partly motivated by Cowen's charisma. To my surprise, he hired me as a research assistant. I only worked for him for one year, and I was not all that much help to him. Nevertheless, he included me on a couple of research papers, and I gave my first public presentation at the 1967 meeting of the Eastern Psychological Association, in Boston. Emory Cowen was always generous with the intellectual credit he gave his students. I learned from him that shared working relationships and intellectual credit are not limited resources. I hope I have been as generous with my own students, but frankly, Cowen was a hard act to follow. After I left graduate school he became my professional father. He always seemed to be looking out for me.

COMMUNITY MENTAL HEALTH
AND COMMUNITY PSYCHOLOGY ENTER MY LIFE

What changed the course of my career was not anything I learned as a research assistant. Indeed, although I learned some skills, I found the work boring, and my own efforts uninspiring. This had nothing to do with Cowen's research, which in many ways was groundbreaking. It had to do with the fact that we were asking his questions, rather than mine. I was still searching for my place in a field for which I felt increasingly unsuited. During my third year at Rochester our first daughter, Loren, was born (November, 1966). Now I was faced with more responsibilities and less of a sense that I would be able to earn a living in a field I had somehow chosen without knowing much about. The more I learned about clinical psychology the less I liked it. I still would not have guessed that I was destined to become a college professor.

Emory tolerated my low key involvement in his research, although we did have one serious argument. He accused me of not working hard and I accused him (a man of boundless energy) of thinking that in order to be working hard you had to be running around frenetically showing everyone that you were working hard. I still wonder at the fact that after this heated session he did not ask me to leave the program. Instead he gave me an additional task. I am thankful that during my third year in graduate school (1966-1967) Cowen was editing a book, with Elmer Gardner and Melvin Zax, called "Emergent Approaches to Mental Health Problems." The chapter authors had just submitted manuscripts and, much to my surprise, Emory asked me to read them, comment on them, and copy edit them. I had learned a lot about editing manuscripts from the way Emory edited my writing, and this, along with my own style, gave me a chance to actually make serious changes in the writing of the scholars who had submitted papers. Not only did I enjoy that process, but it gave me an opportunity to read, very carefully, the newest ideas about what Emory would refer to as "emergent approaches," as the field of Community Psychology was just forming.

Now I became inspired. Suddenly, my experiences and my reading were coming together in a way that made sense to me. Despite the fact that I had spent the year as his research assistant I did not really know much about Emory's ideas until I read and commented on his own lengthy introduction to the Emergent Approaches volume. I remember arguing with him about certain conceptual issues. Although the content of our argument escapes me, I remember him saying in a moment of exasperation, "When you write your own book you can say whatever you want!" I think it was at that moment that I started writing, at least in my head, the textbook on Community Psychology that would help me put my own take on a field that I now desperately wanted to become a part of. Around this time I started reading people like James Kelly and Seymour Sarason. My head swirled with more ideas than I could handle, but I knew now that these were the kind of ideas that made me want to become a community psychologist. As a student member of the departmental colloquium committee I invited Seymour Sarason to campus, met him at the airport, and listened to him describe the development and activities of the Psycho-Educational Clinic at Yale.

HISTORY CALLS AGAIN

History and autobiography were again inescapably linked. The historical time in which I first encountered the practice of psychology and my personal passion for social justice began to overlap. I had been inspired by the anti-poverty and the civil rights movements, and although as an only surviving son I was exempt from the draft, I participated in Viet-Nam War protests, including a demonstration at the United Nations in 1965, where I was chased by angry counter demonstrators holding American flags. Later, when I had my degree, and the war dragged on, I was able to do psychological evaluations to help people escape the draft. None of this was heroic so much as natural to the times in which I was living as a young person. More importantly, the climate of the times was such that I felt I could write about things I cared about, not simply as ideas, but as personal passions and values, in psychology and social science venues.

Before my fourth and last year in graduate school, 1967-1968, historical events that would stay with me throughout my career had been encountered. Lyndon Johnson's "war on poverty," which would be lost by the time I graduated, nevertheless made me aware that it was possible to combine a career in psychology with an active involvement in local community action. Indeed, it seemed possible to obtain grants to pursue such activities, and to involve myself in local community affairs as a legitimate way of teaching and conducting research. A related influence was Cowen's interest in nonprofessionals, especially older adults and college students, who he had recruited as human service volunteers for Rochester's public schools. The notion that one need not have formal training or degrees to be helpful to others immediately struck me as common sense.

Then, in 1966, Ernest Poser, a research psychologist in Canada, published a paper in which he described taking women undergraduates into a local veterans hospital to work as untrained group leaders with long term hospitalized male patients. There had been some work of this sort earlier, but it was mostly descriptive. Poser's study, published in the *Journal of Consulting and Clinical Psychology,* found improvements on a variety of psychological test measures for the patients who had participated when compared to those who had been given group therapy by the hospital professional staff. I had been to the Rochester State Hospital on several occasions to practice interviews and tests under the supervision of Dr. Tom Irwin, a clinical psychologist who had graduated from Rochester and was now a staff member. It occurred to me that the hospital had some 3000 patients housed in its high rise buildings, most of whom spent their days doing nothing. I had actually found people whose name none of the staff knew, sometimes laying on the bathroom floors, sometimes standing up and rocking like the men in the synagogue, but without a prayer.

MY DISSERTATION

At this time Jack Chinsky and his wife, Vivian, lived in the same apartment building as Arlene, Loren and I. We spent a fair amount of time together and I began to talk to Jack about the Poser study. I was interested in trying to use college undergraduates to improve conditions at the Rochester State Hospital, and Jack became interested in what such an experience might do for the students. We went to talk to Emory about this idea, and he suggested that, because such a project was "high risk" and would require a great deal of work, we do a joint dissertation.[2] He encouraged us to share in the administration of a project that would offer a new course for undergraduates who would be recruited to spend an academic year working at the mental hospital. The three of us developed and taught the course. After a summer pilot study, Jack and I took twelve month New York State Internships working at Rochester State Hospital. We recruited other graduate students to help us supervise the students and test the patients. Ultimately the project involved 32 undergraduates (16 male, and 16 female) and 320 patients (half male and half female) with an average hospital stay of more than 20 years. We randomly assigned 256 of them to a same or opposite sex undergraduate group leader who met with them twice weekly, and 64 to a control group. This project and its effects on both the patients and the students is reported in detail in a book–Rappaport, Chinsky and Cowen, "Innovations in Helping Chronic Patients: College Students in a Mental Institution"–published by Academic Press in 1971. Our editor was Larry Erlbaum, just prior to his leaving Academic to start his own, now well known, publishing company. Among the unexpected things I learned was that many people who resided in mental hospitals were there because they had no place else to go. As I got to know the patients at Rochester State Hospital, and saw many of them improve to the point at which they would have benefitted from living in appropriate community settings, I discovered that the reasons they were not released had more to do with social policy than with their individual problems in living. I started my post graduate career determined to work in the area that seemed to best address that reality: Community Mental Health.

ON BEING AN ASSISTANT PROFESSOR (1968-1972)

I had not planned to become a college professor until I started to write my dissertation. At that time I became convinced that I could do things that mattered to me and also write about them in psychology venues. The experience of describing what I had done at the state hospital was exhilarating. In addition to presenting considerable quantitative analysis, I wrote a chapter that today might be thought of as qualitative, or ethnographic. I found that writing about my experience helped me to understand it. I learned that I enjoyed writing conceptual chapters even more than doing empirical research. Since then I have alternated between theorizing, action research projects and data collection; and I have rediscovered the value of qualitative work. I have been blessed by many students and colleagues whose data analytic skills are far better than mine, and I have benefitted very much from their generous collaboration.

As I was finishing my dissertation I had three job possibilities: Columbia, Howard University Medical School, and the University of Illinois at Urbana-Champaign. I decided I could not afford to live in New York. The Howard job was tempting because they were working in the inner city of Washington D.C., but I was uncomfortable taking a job in a medical school, given my graduate school experience. My visit to Illinois was an experience in being star struck. I met O. Hobart Mowrer, a person I consider to be one of the most important psychologists of the last century, J. McV. Hunt, the intellectual force behind Head Start, and an array of others whose work I had read and thought about: Harry Hake, Charles Eriksen, Charles Osgood, Ray Cattell, Jerry Wiggins and many others. An offer from Illinois was impossible to turn down, although I only expected to stay for a couple of years before returning to the east.

Clinical Psychology at Illinois in those days was dominated by behaviorists. I found the behavioral orientation to be quite compatible with community work, especially those behaviorists who preferred field work to in-the-office interventions. However, the Illinois program had just been site visited by NIMH with regard to their clinical training grants. Like many well established departments they had held a clinical training grant since 1948 (the same type of USPHS grant that had supported me as a graduate student). In addition, led by then Director of Clinical Training, Donald Peterson (who would go on to be the Dean at Rutgers Professional School), they had applied for a second training grant to begin a PsyD program that would run in conjunction with the PhD program.[3]

The NIMH site visitors had advised the department that they needed to hire people with expertise in the new field of community mental health. Autobiography and history meet again! The year before I arrived they had hired C. Scott Moss, from NIMH, as a full Professor, to develop courses in community mental health. I was to be his junior colleague. However, before I arrived on campus he suffered a stroke, and although he appeared to me to be fully recovered, he lost the confidence that he could accomplish what he had wanted to do, and within a couple of years decided to leave the university.

This turned out to be an opportunity for me, even as a young assistant professor, to put my own stamp on the development of community psychology at Illinois. With the help of Morton Weir, a developmental psychologist and newly appointed department head, whose values matched my own, I sought and obtained "hard" money from the state to the university in order to support the development of community psychology training within clinical psychology. My argument was that if all my work were dependent on research grants I would not be able to make and sustain a long term commitment to local community people and grassroots organizations. I did not want to participate in the practice of hit and run psychology in which university people enter a community and stay only until they collect their data or the grant ends, leaving people with no lasting collaborators. This is one of the reasons that I have stayed at Illinois for such a long time. It is probably the most important insight I have had about the nature of university/community collaboration: It should not be dependent on time limited grant funds. It requires an infrastructure of support. These funds have continued throughout my career and supported at various times a community run day care center for teen parents, a neighborhood based graphics program, an outreach social worker to the African American Community, and many graduate assistants who I could give the freedom to pursue their own interests in conjunction with my own.

On various occasions, when I considered leaving Illinois, the commitment to community training was reinforced, including an agreement to keep at least three faculty with a community orientation on the clinical faculty. After some initial battles, during my career I have found my clinical colleagues at Illinois to be genuine allies and my department to be tolerant. My clinical colleagues refer to our program as "clinical/community," and my current colleagues, Mark Aber and Nicole Allen, were trained as community, not clinical psychologists. The Director of our department's Psychological Services Center (which used to be called the Psychological Clinic, a name change that reflects our program's commitment to more than in-the-office treatments) is Thom Moore, a friend who has identified throughout his career with Community Psychology. I also held a long term relationship to the Personality and Social Ecology Program which admitted students who have community interests but who do not want to be in a clinical program. Regardless of research area, the current clinical/community faculty share what I consider to be community psychology values, including a commitment to social justice, an openness to varied methodologies, a highly articulated sense that diversity is important, and a desire to admit an ethnic and racially diverse group of students. On my better days I like to think that I have had a hand in creating such a hospitable environment.

POST GRADUATE SCHOOL PROFESSIONAL EXPERIENCES

Among the most important of my early professional experiences post graduate school was an invitation to attend a series of seminars in New York City, organized in the early 1970's by Robert Reiff, the first President of APA's Division of Community Psychology. These seminars included a number of Reiff's postdoctoral students and Morton Bard, James Kelly, Ramsay Liem, Jerry Osterweil and William Ryan. I was just starting to formulate my own way of thinking about communities and these people had a tremendous impact on my thinking. Reiff's positing of the social order in terms of increasingly complex levels of organization, Kelly's ecological analysis, and Ryan's analysis of victim blaming (which had just been published) had profound effects on my thinking. But as much as the content, just having the opportunity to interact with these more senior people helped me to be less shy about expressing myself back home in my own department. I had found a community of colleagues who valued the same things I did and it made me more certain that I could do psychology this way. I decided that even as an assistant professor I could take some risks, i.e., spend a summer working with high school students in Upward Bound, a program for local teenagers from poor neighborhoods who might become interested in college. I learned to write about such projects rather than to rely only on the data I collected from formal surveys or experiments in order to get my ideas into print. Over the course of my career I have often found that I could write about what I learned from participating in the ordinary activities of life, including time spent with local grassroots groups, churches and other community organizations.

In the 1970's Ed Seidman (who we had recruited away from a job in Canada, where he was doing psychotherapy research) and I began a collaboration with Bill Davidson. Ed and I had obtained a grant from NIMH to study the impact of nonprofessionals in a variety of local settings that we had started as practicum experiences for our students. These practica served as pilot ventures before formalizing them into research projects (a strategy that I have used throughout my career). Bill was officially a graduate student, but he was so mature that he was regarded as a peer from the outset. One of our projects involved diverting adolescents from the legal system, and Bill was involved from the beginning in what became his dissertation. My experiences in that project taught me a great deal about the limits of demonstration research and the value of building long term institutionalized relationships in order to implement organizational change.

MY WORK AT ILLINOIS, POST TENURE

The founding of the *American Journal of Community Psychology* in 1973 was another significant event in legitimizing my professional interests, as was an invitation to speak at the Austin Conference in 1975, where I met a group of young, smart, active and committed community psychologists, including Dick Reppucci and Edison Trickett, for the first time. This was just prior to the completion of my community psychology textbook (published in 1977), and I went to the conference filled with ideas that I had never expressed out loud before. I had been spending my first sabbatical year as a James McKeen Cattell Foundation Fellow, living in San Diego, with no responsibilities other than writing and spending time with my family that now included a second daughter, Amy, born in 1972, the year I was granted tenure. Writing that book changed my vision from community mental health to community psychology as I began to see the limitations of an exclusive focus on mental health, and to organize for myself what had seemed to me to be a very wide ranging (dare I say chaotic) field. Shortly after that, with Ken Maton I began to think about religious communities as settings for doing community work. However, I never gave up my early interest in people suffering from severe and persistent problems in living that get them diagnosed as seriously mentally ill and placed in institutional confinement. I was obsessed with the understanding that many problems are made worse by the mental health system people are forced to contend with. Thus, when in the 1980s I was approached by Con Keogh, a Catholic priest and former mental patient from Australia, and other leaders of a mutual help organization called GROW, that functioned without any professional control, I felt as if the answer to my quest for a genuine community mental health project had fallen into my lap.

The leaders of GROW were first referred to me by Hobart Mowrer, who they had contacted because he was known worldwide to be a believer in self and mutual help. They were interested in establishing themselves in America, and they thought that to do so they would benefit from making their organization known to mental health researchers. Hobart knew of my interest in communities, and he saw GROW as a community. This association was to lead to an NIMH collaborative grant, a lengthy series of studies, and many PhD theses by a group of very bright and very compassionate students who have gone on to pursue their own successful careers.

THE INTERSECTION OF MY PRIVATE AND PUBLIC LIVES

My ideas about empowerment, and more recently about the power of community narratives and personal stories, emerged from the connections between my own personal life and my work. The crux of empowerment for me has always been a belief in the ability of ordinary citizens to make a difference in both their own lives and in the life of their community. Because I have resisted the temptations of becoming a nomadic academic I have had many opportunities to develop relationships with local people in mental health, grassroots community organizations and churches. In recent years, inspired by Thom Moore's willingness to serve on the local school board, I have allowed him to convince me and my students to work in a local school in a working class and traditional African American community. I have learned a great deal from the citizens who care about the education of African American children, and from those students who have decided to do their dissertations in that context. This work has linked me back to my own life growing up in a housing project, not feeling at home in school, and being called a bad bet to go to college.

My theory of narratives emerged from listening to former mental patients tell their own stories in opposition to the narratives of mental health professionals, from listening to the dominant cultural and professional narratives that are told about African American children in public schools, noticing how those narratives differ from the personal stories of the children and their families, and from observing the power of a community narrative in both mutual help organizations and churches. My own religious experiences have made me sensitive to both the dangers and the power of a community narrative to offer meaning for those who seek it. My thinking for the last twenty-five years has been influenced by my religious beliefs and experiences. Arlene and I are both Jewish, and we celebrate Jewish holidays and identities. We have also been active members of a non-denominational, Christian religious community, known as New Covenant Fellowship. Occasionally students have conducted their research in this context, and I have occasionally collaborated with both students and the minister, Ron Simkins, who is a close friend, to describe this multi-racial, multi-ethnic community.[4] We also spent five years in a liberal protestant denominational church committed to social justice, and I have written about that community in order to illustrate my thinking about community narratives.[5] Although many people would assert that one cannot be both Jewish and Christian, we are (not always, but usually) comfortable asserting identities that cross expected boundaries. This attitude seems to have been passed on to our daughters, who both married men with quite different family backgrounds than their own. Loren married Caesar, an Italian Catholic, and their children are fair skinned and blue eyed. Amy's husband, Alexander, is Chinese. Their children are obviously Asian, or Eurasian. I am thankful to have lived in a time and place when I could find friendship and meaning among a diverse group of friends, and for the wife who gave me daughters who gave me grandchildren who have increased my own experience of religious and ethnic diversity. I am thankful for the particular ways that my autobiography has met history and led me into unexpected places.

ON BEING AN INSIDER/OUTSIDER: AUTOBIOGRAPHY AND HISTORY REVISITED

As I have reflected on this account, and responded to editorial feedback asking me for certain clarifications, it occurs to me that the story I have rendered (constructed?) contains a certain narrative truth. My life experiences, which I understand to be at the intersection of autobiography and history, make most sense to me (that is, they "feel" right) when I view myself as having been prepared to be an insider/outsider. History has taken my autobiography to the margins. My childhood family life was lived as both observer and participant (what Fay and Ben discussed at night as they planned their next argument required me to act the part of mediator until I was old enough to escape). I had more than one father and chose (or was told) to identify with the one I knew hardly at all. I have lived in completely different neighborhoods and schools, and had a number of alienating educational experiences. Ironically, these experiences have prepared me for the sort of work I do. I was not brought up to be a college professor, a Christian, or a collaborator with people of color; but I am all those things. I am also white, Jewish, and irrevocably working class, although my sister tells me I am an intellectual. I dislike schools and the professionalization of education and helping; but I am a member of an educational establishment in a field that thinks of itself as among the "helping professions."

Fortunately, community psychology has offered me a place where it is permissible to stand outside of what one is in. One attraction of community psychology for me has been its openness to social and self critique, and to the use of my own life experiences as material for understanding, research and action. I find that I can shift perspectives very easily, but not (I don't think) disingenuously. I have often participated in a setting, organization, or community, fully immersed one moment and standing outside of it the next. I am not sure if this is a sense of "marginality," or just a tendency to "go native," and let myself experience different communities of membership. In any case, I find that this is quite natural for me, and also the only way I can actually understand the feel and substance of people and organizations, and at the same time offer a critical outsider's commentary, which I inevitably tend to do. Although I experience life much as I described it intellectually when I wrote, "In praise of paradox,"[6] I am certain that this comes from my life experiences for which I only later found philosophical justification. Perhaps the same can be said for my embracing of qualitative methods and narrative approaches. They both feel congruent with my personality, my autobiography, and the historical forces I have experienced.

NOTES

1. For readers who may want to know more about family life with my step-father, and how, as a young child, I experienced both him and my deceased father, I have written a brief autobiographical short story, titled, "I Am Older Than My Father," that appears in, Pellegrini, R.J., & Sarbin, T.R. (Eds.) (2002) *Between fathers and sons: Critical incident narratives in the development of men's lives.* (pp. 29-37). New York: Haworth.

2. The term "joint dissertation" was Emory Cowen's. At that time, at least in the culture of dissertations at Rochester, Cowen expected that creating an intervention and carrying it out together (conditions he thought necessary to make the project feasible as a practical matter, given the amount of time and responsibilities involved) would be looked upon with skepticism by other faculty. We therefore took pains to clearly demarcate independent questions and data sets, mine focused on the hospital patients and Jack's on the college students. We also had different people on our dissertation committees, although Cowen chaired them both. Today this seems to me to be less unusual, as many graduate students work together on large scale faculty sponsored projects.

3. The Illinois PsyD program admitted students from 1968, the year I arrived, through 1980. The reasons for its demise make for an interesting story, but one that is tangential to this one.

4. Maton, K. I. & Rappaport, J. (1984). Empowerment in a religious setting: A multivariate investigation. In J. Rappaport, C. Swift & R. Hess (Eds.) *Studies in empowerment: Steps toward understanding and action.* (pp. 37-72.) New York: Haworth.

Rappaport, J. & Simkins, R. (1992). Healing and empowering through community narrative. In K. I. Pargament, K. I. Maton & R. Hess (Eds.) *Religion and prevention in mental health: Research, vision, and action.* (pp. 215-236.) New York: Haworth.

5. Rappaport, J. (2000) Community narratives: Tales of terror and joy. *American Journal of Community Psychology, 28,* 1-24.

6. Rappaport, J. (1981) In praise of paradox: A social policy of empowerment over prevention. *American Journal of Community Psychology, 9,* 1-25.

An Accidental Community Psychologist

N. Dickon Reppucci

University of Virginia

SUMMARY. This autobiographical statement discusses personal, contextual and intellectual influences that I perceive as influencing my journey towards developing an identity as a community psychologist. Little was really planned; rather many fortuitous events occurred both in my personal space and in the larger societal context. These somehow interacted and I became an accidental community psychologist. *[Article copies available for a fee from The Haworth Document Delivery Service: 1-800-HAWORTH. E-mail address: <docdelivery@haworthpress.com> Website: <http://www.HaworthPress.com> © 2004 by The Haworth Press, Inc. All rights reserved.]*

KEYWORDS. Gender discrimination, sense of community, serendipity, social contexts, subcultures, social and racial inequities, social support, mentors

I became a community psychologist by accident. My cohort has been referred to as the second generation because we were not among the field's founders, men like Emory Cowen, Ira Iscoe, Jim Kelly, and Seymour Sarason. We attended graduate school in the turbulent 1960s before formal community or community/clinical programs had become commonplace. As a graduate student in the Department of Social Relations at Harvard University (1962-1968), I, like most of my peers, was educated as a clinical psychologist. I arrived in Cambridge at a time when Kennedy's Presidency and its image as Camelot was at its zenith. It was a heady time to be in graduate school, especially to be a member of Harvard's liberal constituency. We were optimistic about society's future and our own. We were caught up in societal events in general, e.g., I marched on Washington in 1963 and heard Martin Luther King deliver his inspirational "I have a dream" speech. However, only a few months later, we heard the news of Kennedy's assassination while in class discussing personality dynamics. The relatively cloistered academic insularity from the world was never more apparent as the professor wanted to continue as though this event was not significant enough to interfere with our discussion. Moreover, the Civil Rights Movement, the numerous urban riots, and the growing war in Vietnam were constant reminders of the inequities in society. Thus, while working to obtain the PhD in a helping profession, these events along with many others of that decade made me realize how far from the action I really was and influenced me to want to be involved with societal as well as individual change.

GRADUATE SCHOOL

The Department of Social Relations was an intellectually stimulating and a creative hybrid as it combined clinical and social psychology with sociology and cultural anthropology. Both my peers and the faculty cared about ideas, and the goal was to be on the cutting edge of new theory and knowledge. Although the term, community psychology, was never uttered, the study of behavior within various contexts was emphasized in several courses, as was the interdisciplinary nature of every social problem. Nevertheless, the treatment interventions we were learning about mainly seemed suited to white, upper class, highly educated, wealthy clients. My initial clinical placement was at the Wellesley Human Relations Services, one of the first community-oriented mental health agencies. At that time, it had the unique notion of offering services in the community, but was less than innovative in its focus on psychoanalytically-based one-on-one therapies. Most of my fellow clinical students were pursuing either a biological/learning or psychoanalytic approach to the understanding of human behavior in order to become either a psychopathology or personality researcher or a clinical practitioner (although the latter was frowned upon). Even though I did not realize it then, I was dissatisfied with all of these approaches, but I had no alternative vision. My year-long assessment course taught by David Marlowe was disillusioning as he emphasized the unreliability and lack of validity of psychological testing and diagnosis. Brendan Maher and Robert Rosenthal (my first advisers) convinced me of the importance of the scientific method, while touting a behavioral/biological approach to treatment (Maher) and the importance of bias, expectancy and context for change (Rosenthal). Gordon Allport stressed the direct approach (versus the unconscious dynamics) for learning about the individual personality, and Robert A. White stressed the understanding of lives in context and the continuum between psychopathology and normality. Meanwhile, Talcott Parsons and David McClelland orchestrated a required year long, interdisciplinary, "meet the stars" course for all the new students in the Department. Parsons, himself, emphasized the influence of the larger macro-systems of society in largely undecipherable lectures and prose, while cultural anthropologists, Beatrice and John Whiting, stressed the importance of culture on individual behavior. Icons–Henry Murray, Eric Erickson and B. F. Skinner (in the psychology department)–were less visible on a daily basis, but their faculty "big man" status enhanced the aura of wisdom and controversy. And during my first year, Timothy Leary's presence on the clinical faculty was a lightning rod for a charged organizational atmosphere. In various ways, all of these professors introduced me to new ideas that required a constant integration and reintegration that very much influenced my developing world view. Moreover, the entire social climate of the Department provided an extremely positive intellectual challenge that was unlike anything I had ever experienced.

As a first year project, I was required to write an extensive interdisciplinary paper on a topic of my own choice that would be evaluated by two independent readers. I chose to tackle prostitution from both a psychological and a sociological perspective. What an eye-opener! Psychologists focused exclusively on intrapsychic phenomena and sociologists exclusively on societal environment. Both were convincing in their own right, but the lack of integration between the theories and perspectives was shocking. It was a powerful learning experience that provided me with a foundation for what has become a rock solid belief that any human problem requires an understanding and appreciation of the individual in context.

I passed general comprehensive exams in psychology and specific exams in psychopathology at the end of my second year (1964) and completed the equivalent of a master's thesis on personality differences between clinical and social psychology graduate students and their career choice–a search of sorts for my own identity. During my third year, I asked a new faculty member, Jerome Kagan, to allow me to be his teaching assistant in developmental psychology and new horizons opened up regarding my understanding of normal development and the longitudinal research method. Moreover, Jerry became my role model for being an exciting and dynamic teacher. I spent the better part of my third year (1964-1965) trying to develop a dissertation proposal on childhood autism as a way of bringing my clinical and developmental interests in children together in a design that would satisfy both Jerry and Norman Watt, a psychopathologist, so that they would agree to be Co-advisers. This effort failed as ideas that seemed stimulating to one of them seemed to leave the other cold. As a result, I left for a year-long clinical internship at the Palo Alto Veterans Administration (VA) Hospital without even a dissertation proposal in hand.

During the year (1965-1966) at the VA, I concentrated on treating individuals with extreme psychopathology, and spent the last 6 months on the maximum security (locked) unit, which was the model for Ken Kesey's ward in *One Flew Over the Cuckoo's Nest*. (Kesey had been an attendant on the ward a few years before I arrived and apparently had often come to work high on LSD.) Not only did I see World War II and Korean War veterans but also some of the first psychological casualties of the Vietnam War, several being men of my own age or younger. I had numerous in-house supervisors, the most influential being a psychodynamically-oriented psychiatrist, William Hall, who ran the locked ward and used an amazing amount of commonsense in his therapeutic interventions. In addition, thanks to a VA policy that hired outside academics as supervisors, I had the opportunity to meet regularly with Sheldon Korchin from Berkeley and Walter Mischel from Stanford. What I learned was that no absolute truth seemed to exist, and that multiple perspectives could be brought to bear to explain the behavior of any individual. In addition, it became clear that numerous contextual factors might contribute to the creation of mental illness, e.g., many lonely men returned with depression, delusions and other symptoms on an annual basis during the winter, only to get well again for the warmer summer weather. I also learned that all of the research knowledge that I had accumulated about psychopathology (and I had a lot) was largely useless in helping me to understand and treat any individual person. Individual interventions, in all but the most circumscribed instances, seemed much more an art than a science. Nevertheless, I became committed to becoming a clinical psychologist as I was fascinated by individual dynamics and the intensity of the process of psychotherapy.

One other very important insight developed as the result of a consultation project that I participated in on several weekends during that year. Jerry Kagan asked me to conduct a series of extensive semi-structured interviews with matched adolescent pairs who three years earlier had scored equally well on math achievement tests but now were either one standard deviation above or one standard deviation below the mean on these tests. Objective personality tests were unable to differentiate the pairs. The project paid well, but it was clearly too big to accomplish by myself. Thus, I asked my apartment-mate, David Reichard, a friend, who had dropped out of the graduate program in social psychology the year before to assist me. He had gone to California to become a statistical consultant with IBM, and he was brilliant. We each tape-recorded two to three hour long interviews with individual youth (4 apiece on at least 6 weekends in Fresno), and planned to transcribe them later. The only systematic difference we had noted was that my interviews tended to be longer than his, but this seemed of little consequence. When the data collection was over, we decided to develop a coding system by listening to several of each other's tapes. It was immediately obvious that I had asked lots of follow-up questions to students' comments while David had not. Why had he not asked what had seemed so obvious to me as follow-up questions? An all-night, heated discussion with David continually making cogent arguments resulted in an important insight, that my facts about people's behaviors were really no more than learned hypotheses that I had incorporated as accurate interpretations of reality. In other words, I had learned to view human behavior through a certain lens that may or may not have had any validity. Where did truth lie? Ever since, I have been extremely aware that my interpretation of reality, although informed by my training and experiences, is only one of many possible interpretations and not necessarily more accurate than other views. I believe this insight has helped me to value alternative explanations and to search actively for them. Moreover, it has reinforced the idea that any interpretation should be modifiable with new evidence or insight.

On my return to Harvard (1966), I made up my mind to complete a dissertation with a single adviser, Jerry Kagan, and found a topic that interested both of us–impulsivity versus reflectivity in two-year-old children. I chose Jerry because he excited me with his genuine enthusiasm for research, and at the time, I was unsure of my own commitment. In addition, I wanted regular access to him, and what better way to accomplish this than to develop a research plan based on ideas central to his own research agenda. The year was spent developing the assessment procedures, in preparation for data collection to begin in the fall of 1966 when the children in Jerry's longitudinal cohort, who had been seen in the lab at age 4, 8, and 13 months, would be 27 months old. My dissertation was an examination of the relationship between the early data and the behavior of the first 50 children at 27 months as well as the relationship between several variables assessed at 27 months. I also had the opportunity to teach my own fall seminar on Clinical Psychopathology which was followed in the spring by a more standard Experimental Psychopathology class. This teaching experience was exceptionally positive, and in conjunction with the research, was significant in helping me decide to pursue an academic career.

In the spring of 1967, Jerry offered me a two year appointment as a Research Associate (September, 1967-August, 1969) to run his lab and oversee the full data collection of the 27-month longitudinal sample in the first year while he took a year-long sabbatical, and then to co-author a planned monograph on the research in the second year. In addition, I would be appointed as a Lecturer in the Department so that I could continue my teaching in psychopathology, which was very important to me. The plan was that I would finish the dissertation in the fall of 1967. Unfortunately, as with many dissertations, it was not completed in the planned timeframe, much to the chagrin of the Department's Associate Chairperson, George Goethals. Moreover, it probably would not have been completed until late spring of 1968 except that in late January, I received a 1A draft notice ordering me to report for processing in 28 days, an all too common experience at the time. At first, this seemed only a small worry as deferrals for teachers were standard if an official letter was sent confirming that the person was essential to the teaching mission of the school. However, Goethals would only write such a pro forma letter when I had turned in my dissertation. This spur to action was duly heeded, and 22 days later the dissertation was finished. I had learned yet again the powerful effect that context can have on behavior, and I obtained the much desired deferral from military service in Vietnam.

What happened next was critical to my becoming a community psychologist. A few short weeks after completing the dissertation, Jerry rapped on my office door and said Seymour is on the phone. My response was Seymour who? His answer, Seymour Sarason, of course. He wants you to interview for a faculty position at Yale. Since I had never applied for this job, and since my wife and I were very happy living in Cambridge, I became quite paranoid. Was this a plot to keep me from co-authoring the book that I viewed as a solid launching pad to an academic career? Or was it Jerry providing an unexpected opportunity? Data collection was clearly going to be finished by early summer. I did not want to interview for the job at all. However, after consultation with a few other faculty members, it was suggested that if I was a "serious" psychologist, I really had to interview for this position. I went to Yale with the firm conviction that I would be interviewed and rejected, and then could continue on as planned. Wrong! I met Seymour and the various faculty and students at the Psycho-Educational Clinic, and by the time I left New Haven, I was sold. Seymour asked the sorts of questions, and we discussed topics in a way that had an electrifying effect upon me. A new field known as community psychology was questioning the status quo of our society, of the clinical profession as it currently existed, and of psychology in general. It stressed active involvement in community settings with broader focus than individual psychotherapy as the method of intervention. All of my interdisciplinary training seemed to come into focus, and I realized that I definitely wanted to investigate and be involved with institutional as well as individual change. Luckily, I was offered the position at Yale and accepted for the fall of 1968.

FAMILY BACKGROUND

Before moving on to the Yale days, I need to note briefly my family background, as I think it influenced many of my perceptions about important aspects of context and human behavior. I grew up in a poor family. My father (Nicholas Ralph Reppucci) was the youngest son of immigrants from Naples, Italy, who settled in the North End of Boston, at the time and for most of the last century, Boston's Italian ghetto. It was a rough, poor neighborhood where few children finished high school. My father was no exception as his formal education ended in the seventh grade when he was permanently expelled from the public school system for punching a school principal. Besides his father had recently died, and he felt that he needed to make money to assist the family. I say make rather than earn because he did not obtain a regular job until I was born in 1941 when he was 33 years old and joined the Teamsters Union. He was a loud, physically powerful and attractive man. Although I have no really accurate picture as to what he did during his pre-teamster days, my impression is that he was a gambler, an excellent pool player, a con and sham artist, and not at all above breaking the law, all of which were totally acceptable in the Italian, low income subculture of which he was a member. I was the first and only son with the Reppucci surname, and this was extremely important to his entire large extended family.

My father met my mother (Bertha Elizabeth Williams) in a speakeasy where she was a waitress and singer. Betty, as she was called, became his third wife, but was from a very different social background. Her formal education had also ended early (eighth grade) because her parents had come upon hard financial times. When she was 13, her family moved from Summit, New Jersey, to Kennebunkport, Maine, where they had previously spent summers. Her mother was a college educated writer of children's stories, who refused to send her children to the Maine public schools, preferring to educate them at home because the public schools were not "good enough." Her father was a painter/illustrator and her parents were part of a social strata of writers and artists, some of whom were very well known, e.g., Booth Tarkington and Kenneth Roberts, and were regular dinner guests. My mother ran away from home at age 18 to marry a lobster fisherman but left that marriage a few years after her first child, my half-sister, Ann, was born. She then left Maine, taking Ann with her, to become a teacher in a private school in Massachusetts. She found being a single mother an impossible economic burden, and therefore, decided to leave Ann with her parents to raise. She always regretted this decision, but at the time, she thought it was in Ann's best interests. She then became a waitress because it paid better than being a school teacher.

My parents were a study of opposites. She was very well read and always had a book underway; he read little besides the newspaper. He enjoyed gambling, especially at cards; she never gambled, although she loved to play bridge. She valued education; he did not. She spent large amounts of time reading to me, taking me to museums, engaging me in various activities; he was seldom home and we spent little time together. They were divorced when I was 11, after 17 years of marriage. My mother, younger sister (Karen) and I moved to Hollywood, Florida, because of Karen's health problems (severe asthma attacks) and so that my mother could make more money as a waitress because of the tourist industry. Even with a modest amount of continued financial support from my father, we could only afford to rent a very small two rooms with bath, guest house. I still remember the embarrassment of having a care package of groceries delivered to our home from the local department of social services when I was in the eighth grade, and of my mother being told by a church elder that he had donated a suit that would probably fit me to the church relief fund–I refused to even consider wearing it. I assumed a fair amount of responsibility when I was 12, taking care of Karen every evening while mother was working as we could not afford a babysitter. At 16, I obtained my first full time summer job. I joined the Carpenter's Union and became an apprentice to two carpenters building the first shopping center in West Hollywood, Florida. These men probably wished they had never met me as I knew nothing, e.g., I did not even know what a 2×4 was when I started and was basically incompetent even at the most menial tasks. Moreover, other than the money I earned ($1.55 an hour) which was almost double what most of my peers were earning, I hated the daily heavy labor in the hot sun. The immediate benefit was that it convinced me that I had to find a way to go to college. The long-term benefit is that it provided a basis of comparison and a sense of humility as to how lucky I am to have been an academic for the past 35 years.

Throughout all of this, I was an avid reader, did extremely well academically at South Broward High School (a large, 1800 student enrollment, segregated, regional high school), and was a participant in numerous extracurricular activities. I loved high school, was part of a very close-knit group of male and female friends on the tennis team, and in my senior year, was President of the Student Government. This latter role was a surprise in that I had been suddenly elevated to this key position of leadership and responsibility. I say suddenly because I had won an election in the spring of my junior year to become First Vice-President (a relatively meaningless position), not President. However, during the summer, the President-elect had eloped with his sophomore sweetheart, and the school administration stripped him of the presidency as he was no longer considered a proper role model. For me, being thrust into this leadership position turned out to be very good training for learning about organizations, teamwork and public articulation of goals, and I thrived on it.

My mother always encouraged me to plan on college, regardless of our financial woes. Moreover, my closest friends were mainly a college-bound group. Several of my teachers were also catalysts: my Latin teacher, Louise Wethington, my English teacher, Elizabeth Waldenmaire, and especially, my civics and American history teacher, Catherine Dinnen, who inspired me not only in the subject matter but also by serving as a role model for the teaching profession. Thus, thanks to a devoted mother, a group of supportive peers, encouraging teachers, several small scholarships that I received at graduation, and a father who provided a small amount of financial support, I became the first Reppucci ever and the first of my extended family to attend college since my maternal grandmother had done so more than 60 years earlier.

Before moving on, I think it is important to note that I was totally unaware of any injustice regarding being in a segregated school system. Although we had moved to Hollywood from the North as had most of my fellow classmates, we spent no time thinking about or really being conscious of the fact that we were in an all white school. Looking back on this, it is hard to imagine how unaware I was of the reality of segregation. In fact, this linkage to my own existence did not really hit me until almost two decades later when I found an old newspaper in a trunk that had pictures of my graduating class in it and on the back page was a picture of the graduating class of the all Black high school that I hardly knew even existed. My only excuse for this egregious unawareness and lack of social consciousness was that the culture of the South (even South Florida with its mainly northern population) was so all encompassing that neither I, nor my classmates, ever questioned it! However, this discovery along with my move into community psychology with its emphasis on understanding human behavior in social context increased my desire to comprehend how people become so embedded in the taken-for-grantedness of their world that they often cannot see it clearly and how they come not just to accept but even to defend a host of unsupportable injustices. With this insight, I became an advocate for examining the histories of people, institutions and the societal forces extant at any given time in order to help us to recognize our own blindnesses, our processes of rationalization and self-justification, and the contingencies linking our lives, beliefs and social worlds (see Reppucci & Saunders, 1977). This historical perspective has permeated both my action and scholarly work to this day.

UNDERGRADUATE EDUCATION

I began my undergraduate career at the University of Florida (free tuition), but was unhappy with the large impersonal environment and having to take ROTC. In addition, I felt sorry for myself for not having pursued any other college options because of the cost of applications and because I assumed that even if I had been accepted, I could not afford to go. Only upon graduation did I learn that a fellow student, whose credentials were no better than my own but whose parents were knowledgeable about the application process, had received a full fellowship to Princeton, the school that I had fantasized about attending. My closest friend, Jerome Tognoli, was also unhappy for several of the same reasons, and we decided to apply to transfer to the University of North Carolina (UNC) at Chapel Hill the next year. UNC was appealing because our high school English teacher had often mentioned it as being a wonderful place, and because a psychology faculty member at Florida, whose name I do not remember, had suggested that it was a very good and affordable school for studying psychology. Although I had never taken a psychology course, I had decided that psychology would probably be my major. I wanted to understand people! Both Jerome and I were accepted to UNC for our sophomore year. UNC turned out to be very affordable (i.e., $80 tuition per semester, and three meals daily for $1 at the University cafeteria) and to have an excellent psychology department. Moreover, after one semester, I received full tuition scholarships for the rest of my time there, and by working as a dormitory advisor in exchange for free housing my junior and senior years, I was able to make a go of it.

UNC turned out to be a "liberal" outpost in a very conservative southern state, and I soon became very aware of the racial turmoil that was beginning to envelop the entire country. A political science course that I took focused on a North Carolina political campaign for the U.S. Senate in which Dr. Frank Graham, the former beloved President of UNC and a liberal politician, was defeated by a candidate who ran a notoriously racial campaign against him. I wish I could say that this new awareness was translated into action, but other than boycotting a segregated local movie theatre, I remained relatively uninvolved. However, in the cognitive realm I became very attuned to the issues, and have actively supported the elimination of racial inequities and the movement toward social justice for all minorities ever since.

My years at UNC were very positive, and I felt very lucky to be a "Tarheel." Jerome and I were elected Co-Editors of the University Yearbook for our senior year, which provided us the opportunity to be creative and to shape a diverse group of people into an effective team. An enormous amount of time and energy was devoted to this task, and we loved every minute of it. We were also among the first undergraduate students in the new psychology honors program. Our mentor was John Thibeau, a social psychologist, so we both applied to graduate schools in that area. Jerome did attend the University of Delaware in social psychology and obtained the PhD. I was fortunately accepted with financial support at several places, but chose to enter the clinical psychology program in the Department of Social Relations at Harvard. Not only was I surprised at being accepted (I had applied to Harvard mainly so that I wouldn't have regrets as I did about Princeton), but also because I had been accepted in social psychology at the other schools. Being naive and in awe of the Harvard mystique, I assumed the Admissions Committee had seen something in my application that suggested that I should be in clinical rather than social psychology and had given them great insight into my very being. In actuality, it was a lucky event because I obviously had no idea what I wanted, and I had the opportunity to pursue this area with few, if any, pre-conceived ideas. Thus, while several of my peers were somewhat dissatisfied with the program, I enjoyed everything. The fit between the program and myself was very positive. Still, it took me more than a year to stop thinking of myself as an admissions error (almost all of my Harvard peers had gone to Ivy League or elite small Mid-Western or Northeastern colleges). By the time, I went to Yale I had grown in confidence and was ready for a new challenge, and the name of that challenge was Community Psychology.

CHRISTINE

Another extremely important event occurred in my life in September, 1967. I married Christine Marlow Onufrock, a fellow Harvard graduate student, a year ahead of me in the clinical program. She was also working with Jerry Kagan as her adviser on a behavior genetics dissertation concerned with infants over the time span from 4 to 8 months of age. She and I had been going out for much of the time we were in graduate school but had separated for the year I had been in California on internship. She had become a committed clinical psychologist, and when the Yale opportunity presented itself, she was supportive of my accepting it although it meant she had to give up a very stimulating clinical position at the South Shore Mental Health Center in Quincy, Massachusetts. An important but devastating lesson was then learned. Although the notion of gender discrimination was not new, Christine had never experienced it first hand, and I was not convinced that it even existed. Her credentials were outstanding on all fronts, including an exceptional amount of clinical experience, and she should have been a prime candidate for a demanding clinical position. As it turned out, she applied for a clinical psychology faculty position (three were available) at the Yale Medical Center, and she was invited for an interview with the Director of Clinical Services. With great excitement, we drove to New Haven. Her description of the interview process was shocking in that the Director did not even pretend that she was being seriously considered for one of the positions. He had her come into his office and proceeded to read his mail for about 10 minutes while she sat waiting patiently. He then said something like, "I hear your husband has taken a position in the psychology department, and as a courtesy to Seymour, we need to help find you a job somewhere in New Haven." He did not even talk about the three jobs at the Center; all of which were filled by white males. For her, the experience was hurtful and destructive of her self-esteem. For me, I became critically aware of gender discrimination and have actively sought to alter it over the years.

It is perhaps worth noting that Christine and I have remained married and raised three children–two sons, Nicholas and Jonathan, both attorneys, and Anna, our adopted Korean daughter, a public relations specialist, who has recently made us grandparents. Christine has been and remains both my most valued friend and my most trusted critic. Moreover, she has been a well-respected and full-time professional clinical psychologist for all but a few years when the children were very young.

Perhaps the importance of family deserves emphasis. Although Christine and I have both had full time careers, being parents has been our most important role. By this I mean that being available to the children as they grew up has taken precedence. For me, this meant being home regularly for evening meals, being involved with their schooling and being available to encourage various youth activities, e.g., I coached youth soccer for many years although I knew nothing about the sport, read to them nightly, and took regular family vacations. This involvement clearly meant producing fewer articles than I otherwise might have, but the significance of family was reinforced during my Yale years. This may sound like a contradiction in that there was enormous pressure for me to be productive in publication, and there were few boundaries between work and life in general. However, Seymour Sarason, my intellectual and emotional father and most important mentor, always emphasized family before anything else. Even today, his first inquiries are about Christine and the children, and they are not perfunctory. He really wants to know how their lives are progressing.

THE YALE YEARS

Of course, Seymour was also a role model for my career as an academic. He arrived daily at the Psycho-Educational Clinic early, and by the time I arrived at 8:30 a.m., he had been writing for three hours and was ready for a break. He would invariably invite me into his office for coffee and a ten minute discussion. These morning encounters proved to be among the most intellectually exciting times of my life. Seymour always had a new idea, a new way of looking at an old idea, or a way of motivating me to think. It seemed to me that I had relatively little to say about anything, but Seymour would pounce on something that I said and make it seem as though my comments were of spectacular genius. The fact that I knew this was not the case was immaterial. The first year at the Clinic was like no other before or since. During my first week, Seymour took me to lunch and told me that one of my teaching assignments was to co-teach his undergraduate community psychology seminar. That I knew nothing about this field made no difference; as he said, you know a lot more than you think. He also explained that a post-doctoral fellow had decided not to come to the Clinic and that this meant that this person's consultation assignments at several elementary schools and the high school in the working class town of Derby, Connecticut, had to be shared. My first thought was to wonder what he expected me to do about this. It rapidly dawned on me that I should volunteer to help my boss in a crisis. I offered to try my hand at the high school as I was interested in adolescence, and in fact, was teaching a seminar on that topic. It took me only about ten more minutes before I realized that he expected me to pick up an elementary school too. My protestations that I knew nothing about this age child and that the last time I had been in an elementary school was when I was a student there, made not a dent in his determination to have me do this consultation. He assured me that the school system was not being overcharged for my services, and I had lots of competencies. Seymour's co-authored book (Sarason, Levine, Goldenberg, Cherlin, & Bennett, 1965), *Psychology in Community Settings*, was to serve as my guide, and he would meet with me whenever I wanted him to. Having grown up with the Italian tradition that you scratch my back, and I'll scratch yours, and being able to recognize an offer that I could not refuse, I started my journey toward becoming a community psychologist. The assignments at the two schools turned out to be exciting learning experiences regarding the process of entry, consultation, the dynamics of institutional change, and collaborative interventions. Moreover, I did have a competence in the use of social learning techniques to change behavior, and I was good at interacting with the school teachers and administrators. And to my surprise, it was the elementary school that intrigued me the most, and made it easy to relinquish my consultation in the high school to Ed Trickett, when he was hired the next year.

Every Friday morning, 20-22 faculty, graduate students and other members of the Clinic met in the Conference Room to discuss research and action projects, listen to invited academic and community speakers, and raise various issues that had arisen during our forays into the community. Seymour was a spectacular discussion leader, and no topic was off base. The rule of thumb was that every person had to sit around the large conference table, not behind others. As such, each was expected to contribute to the discussions as equals. I remember the time Seymour decided to talk about leisure time, and I thought, what in the world does this have to do with psychology and/or social problems. By the end of the discussion, I was totally immersed in the issue. Another time, he had asked the well-known organizational psychologist, Warren Bennis, then Provost at the University of Buffalo, to discuss candidly what it was like to be doing this job. On another occasion, the eminent developmental psychologist, Arnold Samaroff, presented a slide show of his trip to Prague during the summer of 1968, just before the Soviet crack-down. Although at first glance, these discussions may have seemed almost anti-academic, they actually increased my awareness of the linkage of everyday life with theoretical issues of enduring importance such as the creation of settings, the role of the university in society, and the centrality of people's need for a psychological sense of community. A bond developed between everyone at these meetings. The basic feeling tone was that of an emotional and intellectually curious family–Seymour's family. The implicit and explicit agreement was that we should be honest (not mean) with each other, participate actively, and leave any animosities at the door. It was like nothing I have experienced in academia before or after, and it was amazingly informative and exciting. A true psychological sense of community was nurtured, and I believe that all who were a part of it cherish the experience to this day. It has also had an enduring impact on how I have developed my own research teams, interacted with students, colleagues and friends, and have tried to live my life.

At one of my first Clinic meetings, Ellis MacDougall, the recently appointed Connecticut Commissioner of Corrections, had been invited by Ira Goldenberg, a faculty colleague, to discuss his vision for this new Department. He had brought with him, his Director of Programming and Planning, Charles Dean, a PhD sociologist. MacDougall solicited university involvement, and at the conclusion, I offered my services. He shunted me off to Dr. Dean, and this turned out to be the beginning of a very productive six year collaboration. Dean wanted help with changing either the local, grossly over-populated and ancient, New Haven jail, a hell-hole if there ever was one, or with a new minimal security facility for juveniles to be opened in the near future on a mountaintop an hour's distance from New Haven. Having recruited a team of graduate students to work with me, we opted for involvement with the latter, because its newness seemed like a good omen for a successful intervention. How wrong-headed we were to make this choice, given the context and location of this new setting, only dawned on us about six months into this intervention. We actually wrote a chapter (Reppucci, Sarata, Saunders, McArthur, & Michlin, 1973) on our experiences entitled "We bombed in Mountview: Lessons learned in consultation to a correctional institution for adolescent offenders." Nevertheless, the intervention was significant in that we learned a great deal about juvenile offenders and correctional facilities, and it cemented my relationship with Dean, which led to several other research and intervention projects in the juvenile justice system.

The next year (1969-70), my graduate student team and I spent some time conducting groups for youth who had been convicted of drug crimes at the Cheshire Reformatory for 17-21 year-old boys, and one of my students, Verne MacArthur, focused his dissertation research on the experiences of youth being released from the facility that was published as his book, *Coming Out Cold* (McArthur, 1974). A year later (June, 1970), Dean was appointed Superintendent of the Connecticut School for Boys, the state correctional facility for 12-16-year-old adjudicated male delinquents, and a research team composed of Terry Saunders, Brian Sarata, Lee Wilkinson and myself joined with Dean to change the culture of this facility to one of rehabilitation versus punishment. This four year project, about which we have written much (e.g., Reppucci, 1973; Reppucci & Saunders, 1974, 1978, 1982, 1983; Wilkinson & Reppucci, 1973), was the critical adventure that established my credentials as a community psychologist with expertise in consultation, juvenile justice and behavior modification in the real world. It also served as the explicit stimulus for and precursor of my intensive involvement in the study of children, law and public policy for the past 30 years. Parallel to this venture, several of my other students and I pursued issues related to behavior modification with elementary school children (Steven Reiss, Ronald Kaplan), demonstrating the applicability of the concept of learned helplessness to children's behavior (Carol Dweck) and depression (Ross Rizley), and investigating regularities in the schools (Rhona Weinstein on the impact of reading groups in the first grade) and in other human service institutions (Brian Sarata on job satisfaction in institutions for the mentally retarded; Terry Saunders on learning networks among administrators of juvenile correctional facilities, elementary school principals, and directors of centers for the mentally retarded). In these endeavors, I participated as an active collaborator, with the graduate students, and much enjoyed the camaraderie and sense of shared excitement. These experiences led me to the realization that my favorite part of being an academic community psychologist was my interaction with and mentorship of graduate students. This has remained true throughout my career. I also realized that what was special about community psychology was its wide-ranging, ecological perspective with its focus on both the individual and context, strengths vs. weaknesses, prevention vs. cure, valuing diversity, and the importance of history, social forces, and personal experiences in the formation of our values. I could truly embrace its core co-equal values of seeking knowledge for the sake of understanding and using that knowledge for the sake of action.

Another critical experience during these years was being invited to attend the Austin Conference on Training in Community Psychology in 1974. It was at this meeting that I met Richard Price, Julian Rappaport and other contemporaries with whom I developed positive working relationships and friendships over the years. In fact, this extended network has been crucial to my commitment to the field and was instrumental to an idea (shared with Ed Seidman and Jean Ann Linney) that the field needed a regularly occurring conference to enhance its psychological sense of community and commitment. As a result, 12 years later, when I became President of the Community Psychology Division, my lasting (hopefully) contribution to the field was to orchestrate the initiation of the Biennial Conferences that have become a mainstay for the organization.

THE VIRGINIA YEARS

By the time I left Yale in 1976 to become a Professor and Director of a new Clinical program in the Psychology Department at the University of Virginia (UVA), my identity as a community psychologist was complete, although I remained greatly involved with clinical issues. At this time, I was also the father of two sons and Christine and I were in the process of adopting our daughter from Korea. Several years previously, we had picked out UVA as one of the few places in the country where we would really like to move because of its academic reputation, its location in a family-friendly community, and my fond memories of Chapel Hill, a town that seemed similar in many ways to Charlottesville. Thus when the opportunity arose, we were excited about the move and the future. The Department of Psychology was clearly in a phase of rapid expansion and during the past five years had committed itself to establishing programs in developmental, social and clinical psychology. Thus, I would be in a leadership position that would allow me great influence about the design and shape of the clinical program, and the Chair, James Deese, assured me of the support for a focus on community, children, families, prevention and public policy. It was an exciting new challenge.

From the beginning, however, students could opt to focus on community psychology only, thereby eliminating the focus on individual assessment and psychotherapy as the intervention of choice, as well as the necessity of a clinical internship and other requirements for licensing which were clearly forthcoming. This option became critical as a result of conflicting views between a new department chair and myself regarding the focus of the clinical program. Thus, in 1980, I relinquished the role as director of a clinical training program that promised to become more traditional in its focus on psychopathology, and became director of the free-standing community program. I have served continuously in this role ever since. Although the community program has remained linked to the clinical program, it has often been more integrated with our developmental program. In fact, from 1997-2001, I served as Director of our NIMH developmental training grant. It is probably also worth noting that I served as the initial Director of Graduate Studies in the Psychology Department for the 11 year period 1984-1995. During this time, the community program became one of the seven core departmental areas, although clearly viewed by many faculty members as less central than the other six (clinical, cognitive, psycho-biology, social, developmental and quantitative). The program has survived in large part because of the quality of the graduate students who have matriculated and the subsequent exceptional academic and other placements they have achieved.

The community program has always been small (approximately two new students annually), and today consists of myself and four other faculty members, Charlotte Patterson, Joseph Allen, Nancy Weinfield and Melvin Wilson, the current President of the Society for Community Research and Action. All of us are also core faculty of the developmental and/or clinical areas. Our goal is to educate a committed core of community psychology researchers and teachers. Emphasis is given to ensuring that students have solid methodological and quantitative skills in order to enable them to become faculty members at major research universities. There is a commitment to diversity, an interdisciplinary perspective, and community collaboration. Throughout their time in graduate school, students are involved in research and action projects in community settings and they have an obligation to integrate and conceptualize psychological research in a fashion that may have an impact on public and/or legal policy. My own work has focused on the impact of the legal context on children and families (e.g., Reppucci, Mulvey, Weithorn & Monahan, 1984), emphasizing child abuse (e.g., Haugaard & Reppucci, 1988; Reppucci & Fried, 2000), especially its prevention (e.g., Reppucci, Britner & Woolard, 1997; Reppucci & Haugaard, 1988), and juvenile justice and adolescent development (e.g., Reppucci, 1999), intervention (e.g., Tate, Reppucci & Mulvey, 1996) and public policy (e.g., Trivits & Reppucci, 2002). Current major intellectual and action emphases in my lab include adolescent decision making in legal contexts, female delinquency and aggression, police interrogation of juveniles, public perceptions of adolescent culpability, and restorative justice interventions with juveniles. Among my PhDs from the Virginia program who have ended up in academia/research are Ed Mulvey (University of Pittsburgh Medical Center), Mindy Rosenberg (Adjunct, University of California, Berkeley), Jennifer Kofkin Rudkin (University of Denver), Mark Aber (University of Illinois, Champaign), Jeffrey Haugaard (Cornell), David Scherer (University of New Mexico), Michael Arthur (University of Washington), Michael Blank (University of Pennsylvania), Sarah Cook (Georgia State University), Sharon Portwood (University of Missouri, Kansas City), Jennifer Woolard (Georgetown University), Cathy Crosby-Currie (St. Lawrence University), Preston A. Britner IV (University of Connecticut), Richard Redding (Villanova Law School and Hanneman Medical School), Camille Preston (Police Executive Research Forum, Washington, DC), Frances Lexcen (University of Massachusetts Medical Center), and Deborah Land (Johns Hopkins). I am proud of these students and their accomplishments, and I hope that my most important legacy is that I helped them to think better. (Note: I have mentored many other students and am equally proud of their accomplishments in the more applied spheres.)

CONCLUSION

For me, the essence of being a community psychologist is viewing social problems through an ecological lens and using the scientific method to study them. It is also being aware of one's own limitations, and collaborating with individuals from other disciplines to work on social problems, e.g., I have collaborated with Elizabeth Scott, Professor of Law, for several decades, and I am the better for it. I advocate reading the following papers for a more detailed exposition of what I hold to be the critical foundation for the field. Jim Kelly's 1971 seminal article on "Qualities for a Community Psychologist" spells out several of the required prerequisites for being successful, not the least of which are pursuing interdisciplinary interaction, adopting a longitudinal perspective, and having a distinct competency, a toleration for ambiguity, and a willingness to give the by-line away. Julian Rappaport's (1983) article "In Praise of Paradox: A Social Policy of Empowerment Over Prevention" and Seymour Sarason's 1974 book, *The Psychological Sense of Community: Prospects for a Community Psychology,* provide powerful value statements. My 1985 paper on "Psychology in the Public Interest" defines general methods and goals that I advocate for the field, including confrontation with the dilemma of values. Seymour Sarason's 1972 *The Creation of Settings and the Future Societies* (the single most important book in our field) provides a framework for understanding individual, organizational and societal change, and several of his provocative *American Psychologist* papers, most importantly "Community Psychology, Networks and Mr. Everyman," "Psychology Misdirected" and "Psychology *To The Finland Station* in *The Heavenly City of the Eighteenth Century Philosophers,*" help us to avoid fool's gold and the all too prevalent attitude of professional preciousness. Lastly, Judge David Bazelon's 1973 address to the American Psychological Association requesting that psychologists be actively involved with the public interest but that they reveal their often times hidden biases and values when presenting their data for public consumption should be required reading for all community psychologists. I believe that these are the most essential readings and convey best the importance of our field when it is practiced with honesty and commitment.

    I believe that the critical threads for many of my views have their roots in my family of origin, my good fortune at being able to achieve a college education at all and then at being accepted to an intellectually stimulating graduate department at a time of intense social turmoil in American society, where I not only developed the basis for critical thinking but also found my life's intellectual and emotional partner. Then, my accidental discovery of and entry into the newly emerging field of community psychology with its explicit value of using knowledge for the public good was bolstered by eight years of intense mentorship from Seymour Sarason and the development of collaborative relationships with several challenging graduate students in an atmosphere that demanded excellence but also insisted that I find my own voice. By the time I became a Professor at the University of Virginia, I understood the benefits of a demanding academic environment and was ready to undertake the creation of a new training program that would have as its focus the advancement of knowledge for the public interest. For me, the essence of training in community psychology consists of defining the parameters of any given social problem and asking the critical questions. This usually means recognizing that several possible solutions to the same social problem often exist simultaneously, that the preferred solutions may be based on both science and values, and that solutions viable at one time in history may become undesirable at another time. Community psychologists must have a tolerance for ambiguity, and like politicians, be able to accept and to help others to accept compromise. Community psychology's goal is to help make our society a better place to live. To do this means embracing diversity and accepting the idea that a science of human behavior in context is probably our best bet for achieving this goal. But just as science is always changing because of the discovery and integration of new knowledge, we need to be open to incorporating this knowledge into new frameworks even if they are not isomorphic with our own values.

Whether this essay sheds any light on the development and creation of the field of community psychology, I leave to Jim Kelly and others to evaluate. I am too close to the material to know. However, I do know that it has been an intriguing exercise to write this essay!

REFERENCES

Bazelon, D. L. (1982) Veils, values and social responsibility. *American Psychologist,* 37, 115-121.

Haugaard, J.J., & Reppucci, N.D. (1988). *The sexual abuse of children: A comprehensive guide to current knowledge and intervention strategies,* San Francisco: Jossey-Bass.

Kelly, J. (1971) Qualities for the community psychologist. *American Psychologist,* 26, 897-903.

McArthur, A.V. (1974) *Coming out cold: Community reentry from a state reformatory,* Lexington, MA: D.C. Heath & Company.

Rappaport, J. (1983) In praise of paradox: A social policy of empowerment over prevention. *American Journal of Community Psychology* 9, 1-26.

Reppucci, N.D. (1985) Psychology in the public interest. In A.M. Rogers and C.J. Scheier (Eds), *The G. Stanley Hall Lecture Series, Volume 5,* Washington, DC: American Psychological Association.

Reppucci, N.D. (1999) Adolescent development and juvenile justice. *American Journal of Community Psychology,* 27, 307-326.

Reppucci, N.D., Britner, P., & Woolard, J. (1997). *Preventing child abuse and neglect through parent education*. Baltimore: Paul Brookes.
Reppucci, N.D., & Fried, C. (2000) Child abuse and the law. *UMKC Law Review*, 69, 107-125.
Reppucci, N.D., & Haugaard, J.J. (1989) The prevention of child sexual abuse: Myth or reality. *American Psychologist*, 44, 1266-1274.
Reppucci, N.D., Mulvey, E., Weithorn, L., & Monahan, J. (Eds.) (1984). *Children, mental health and the law*. Beverly Hills, CA: Sage
Reppucci, N.D., Sarata, B.P.V., Saunders, J.T., McArthur, A.V., & Michlin, L. (1973). We bombed in Mountville: Lessons learned in consultation to a correctional institution for adolescent offenders. In I.I. Goldenberg (Ed.), *The helping professions in the world of action*. Lexington, MA: D.C. Heath & Company.
Reppucci, N.D., & Saunders, J.T. (1974). The social psychology of behavior modification: Problems of implementation in natural settings, *American Psychologist*, 29, 649-660.
Reppucci, N.D., & Saunders, J.T. (1977). History, action, and change. *American Journal of Community Psychology*, 5, 399-412.
Reppucci, N.D., & Saunders, J.T. (1978). Innovation and implementation in a state training school for adolescent delinquents. In R. Nelson and D. Yates (Eds.), *Innovation and implementation in public organizations*, Lexington, MA: D.C. Heath & Company.
Reppucci, N.D., & Saunders, J.T. (1982). Measures of staff morale and organizational environment as indicators of program change in an institution for youthful offenders. In A. Jeger and R. Slotnick (Eds.), *Community mental health and behavioral ecology: A handbook of theory, research, and practice*. New York: Plenum, 171-186.
Reppucci, N.D., & Saunders, J.T. (1983) Focal issues for institutional change. *Professional Psychology: Research and Practice*, 14, 514-528.
Sarason, S.B. (1972) *The creation of settings and the future societies*. San Francisco: Jossey-Bass.
Sarason, S.B. (1974) *The psychological sense of community: Prospects for a community psychology*. San Francisco: Jossey-Bass.
Sarason, S.B. (1975) Psychology *To the Finland Station* in *The Heavenly City of the Eighteenth Century Philosophers. American Psychologist*, 30, 1072-1080.
Sarason, S.B. (1976) Community psychology, networks, and Mr. Everyman. *American Psychologist*, 31, 317-328.
Sarason, S.B. (1981) An asocial psychology and a misdirected clinical psychology. *American Psychologist*, 36, 827-836.
Sarason, S.B., Levine, M., Goldenberg, I.I., Cherlin, D.L., & Bennett, E.M. (1966). *Psychology in community settings: Clinical, educational, vocational, social aspects*. New York: Wiley.
Tate, D., Reppucci, N.D., & Mulvey, E. (1995). Violent juvenile delinquents: Treatment effectiveness and implications for future action. *American Psychologist*, 50, 777-781.
Trivits, L., & Reppucci, N.D. (2002). Application of Megan's law to juveniles. *American Psychologist*, 57, 690-704.
Wilkinson, L., & Reppucci, N.D. (1973). Perceptions of social climate among participants in token economy and non-token economy cottages in a juvenile correctional institution. *American Journal of Community Psychology*, 1, 330-341.

Our Paradigms, Ourselves: Reflections on the Ecology of a Community Psychologist

Edison J. Trickett

University of Illinois at Chicago

SUMMARY. The paper reflects on the life experiences that influenced both my involvement in folk music and my career as a community psychologist. In particular, the role of chance, supportive adults and social settings, travel, and encounters with diversity served to turn the ongoing experience of personal and professional marginality into a resource for me over time. The paper's title reflects my understanding of how my ecological perspective, developed over the years in community psychology, is rooted in critical life events and happenstance occurrences. This reflection has helped clarify the visceral connection between the ecological contexts of my personal/professional experiences and Jim Kelly's initial presentation of the ecological metaphor for the field. *[Article copies available for a fee from The Haworth Document Delivery Service: 1-800-HAWORTH. E-mail address: <docdelivery@haworthpress.com> Website: <http://www.HaworthPress.com> © 2004 by The Haworth Press, Inc. All rights reserved.]*

Address correspondence to: Department of Psychology (M/C 285), University of Illinois at Chicago, 1007 W. Harrison Street, Chicago, IL 60607.

[Haworth co-indexing entry note]: "Our Paradigms, Ourselves: Reflections on the Ecology of a Community Psychologist." Trickett, Edison J. Co-published simultaneously in *Journal of Prevention & Intervention in the Community* (The Haworth Press, Inc.) Vol. 28, No. 1/2, 2004, pp. 63-80; and: *Six Community Psychologists Tell Their Stories: History, Contexts, and Narrative* (eds: James G. Kelly, and Anna V. Song) The Haworth Press, Inc., 2004, pp. 63-80. Single or multiple copies of this article are available for a fee from The Haworth Document Delivery Service [1-800-HAWORTH, 9:00 a.m. - 5:00 p.m. (EST). E-mail address: docdelivery@haworthpress.com].

KEYWORDS. Ecology, social support, autobiography, narrative

The charge to talk about oneself and one's career provides an opportunity for public reflection that many of us are not granted. I appreciate this opportunity. It is evident to me that I write this recollection of the past through the lens of the present. Today I hold all the markers of the "establishment"; a white male raised in the protestant tradition, holding "establishment credentials" of tenured full professor status. I have been educated and taught at some of the premier institutions in the country. I am currently in a wonderful position, heading a Community and Prevention Research program that is one of the strongest in the country. I am able to devote most of my professional time to do the work that I love. As always, I travel and play folk music in different parts of the country. And, most importantly, I spend both quantity and quality time with my family: Dina, and our two children Nicholas and Alexander. My professional collaboration with Dina continues to evolve and deepen my appreciation of the lives and struggles of immigrants and refugees as well as the institutions on whom they depend. My two daughters from my first marriage are also doing well, Jennifer as a public school teacher and Kate as a recent graduate of both college and chef school and wide receiver on a women's professional football team in California.

Professionally, I've had one and a half callings, one as a community psychologist and a half as a folk musician, playing professionally but not on the road full time. Both of these lives have been linked to a deep appreciation for understanding and celebrating the perspective of the "outsider." In fact, despite my "establishment" status, the feeling of marginality has been recurrent and central in my life, as has the excitement of exploration of different ways of life, the satisfaction gained from participating in creating a sense of community, and the nurturing power of supportive social settings. I have also come to appreciate the extent to which chance plays a role in life in ways that cannot possibly be anticipated by "risk factors" or other markers, as my life has involved a series of turns that landed me in places one would not have anticipated given my roots. Where and who I am today has been a result of the interaction, over time, of my own personal history and passions with fields whose individuals and settings have provided me with a lifelong calling. Thus in titling this paper "Our Paradigms, Ourselves," I am reflecting, from the inside, on those influences. My professional life has centered on two movements more closely intertwined than I ever imagined or understood when I first committed to them: the worlds of folk music and community psychology. Both these worlds, shaped inexorably by the 1960s and the consciousness of that decade, have been callings more so than professions or avocations.

My ancestors came to the United States during the Revolutionary War, fighting, as it turned out, on the wrong side. But they decided to stay and, by the turn of the 20th century, found themselves in West Virginia. My grandfather ran away from home at age 10 because, I was told, his father beat him once too often. He learned to be self-sufficient at an early age and, after working odd jobs for several years, married the daughter of the woman who ran the boarding house in which he was staying. He began working in the coal mines, where the family eeked out a subsistence level life in a company town controlled by the mining company. Growing up, I remember him recalling how the coal company would tie wages to the cost of living in the company town so that miners would not be able to save enough money to quit their jobs and move on. He told how the company store was organized to emphasize the cradle-to-grave aspect of the miner's lot, with baby goods on the first floor and coffins on the top. Between stints in the mine, he worked as a labor organizer in southwestern Pennsylvania, and the stories he would tell of the secrecy and stealth necessary to avoid company thugs became part of my understanding of what the world was like. I always admired his courage, commitment, and philosophy about the haves and have-nots that energized him and his work. He was also a professional boxer for a time, with huge hands, red hair, and a quick though usually controlled temper. He knew how to tell a good story, and one of my childhood delights was listening to him describe his real or fictitious (I neither knew nor cared) adventures in the mines, in the ring, or avoiding the company thugs. His descriptions helped me understand the marginality of the powerless, the appreciation of telling the story from the inside, and a sense of which side of the tracks I came from.

My grandparents had seven children, of whom my father was the youngest. My grandfather took my father to the mines with him at an early age, and eventually my father worked there as an alternative to finishing high school. He did well in subjects that interested him, but they were few. I grew to know him as a very caring person with a huge heart and a keen sense of humor. As an adult, he had a variety of jobs reflecting mostly his ability to fix anything in houses or cars. I always thought that between the two of us we were really a pretty well rounded person, with his ability to be useful and my penchant to conceptualize it through formal education and polysyllabic words. But his marriage to my mother was short-lived, and he took me away from her within a couple months of my birth in Uniontown, Pennsylvania and moved me to his parents' house in Washington D. C. While he didn't like to talk about it, he was very concerned about her lack of caring for me as an infant. In a manner typical of the times, my family had moved from West Virginia to Washington after the Depression in piecemeal fashion, with my aunt Margaret leading the way and getting a government job that allowed her to bring the rest of the family to town.

I was raised in my grandparents' home, along with several of their grown children. My father, after returning from World War II (he was a Marine) agreed to let my grandparents adopt me, so I grew up seeing him regularly but not living with him. It was a quite fateful decision, for it inadvertently opened up a world of educational and social opportunities that were fateful in my future. The primary influence over this twist of fate was my aunt Margaret, my grandparents' eldest child who was there throughout my childhood and adolescence and took primary responsibility for raising me. Her unconditional acceptance and love over the course of her 90 years remains both as inspirational as it does inexplicable. Margaret took responsibility for just about everything in the house, including me. She actively crafted my educational opportunities, getting me into a private school at an early age, and even sending me to Arthur Murray's Dance School to learn ballroom dancing so I would know the social graces associated with the private school world. Ironically, Arthur Murray set me apart from rather than integrated me into that world, as I was probably the only kid in school who, at age 13, could do the Mambo, Samba, Tango, and Paso Doble. The bottom line, however, was that Margaret, uncomfortable herself with the world she wanted me to experience, actively created opportunities for me that no one in my family had ever, at the time, thought of as possible. And at every choice point she reaffirmed her belief that I would be able to take advantage of the opportunities she provided.

Looking back, I see in this history a sense of self grounded in the "have/have-not" class distinction, a sense of loss about my early family, as well as a sense, from Margaret, that I had potential. The soul of folk music is in these experiences, although in my home classical music predominated. Margaret was also the source of that as well, a first rate classical pianist whose gentle touch would fill our evenings with the best of Beethoven, Brahms, and Bach. At her insistence, I took up the piano as well when I was five. It took me 8 years to finally talk her out of making me take lessons, and I never totally forgave her for letting me get my way. Her introduction to music, however, would open up an enduring source of pleasure, as would her letting me get my way create a kind of stubbornness and hopefulness about life in general.

Margaret was committed to my education, and it was through that commitment that I ended up at Beauvior School, a private school on the grounds of the Washington Cathedral. It was one of the feeder schools for St. Albans, a premier elite private school founded in the early 1900s to educate boys in the Washington Cathedral Choir. In 2nd grade, I was accepted into the junior choir and, a year later, into the senior choir and admitted to St. Albans with a scholarship that accompanied being a choirboy. Until my boy soprano voice changed sometime later, I had the most wonderful church-based musical education imaginable. The music provided me with an ongoing sense of history, spirituality, and the role of music as a binding expressive force. We practiced 10 hours a week, sang in weekday and Sunday services, and, occasionally, traveled to other cities to sing. The choir provided my first encounter with being on the road, and I have a vivid memory of waking up in a sleeping car traveling through Pennsylvania on the way to a concert in Detroit, seeing a light snow falling silently outside the sleeping car window, and thinking it simply couldn't get much better than this.

While the Washington Cathedral choir allowed access to a wonderful storehouse of religious music covering many centuries, the folk music that would sustain me began during my adolescent years at a summer camp north of Taos, New Mexico. Howard Wilson, a classmate at St. Albans, asked me one spring day about my then non-existent summer plans, and suggested I look into a camp he was going to go to in New Mexico. The idea was appealing. About 50 adolescents and 10 counselors would travel across the country in school buses, camp out at night, and spend the summer in the foothills of the Sangre de Cristo Mountains in a valley populated primarily by Spanish-speaking farmers. I spent part of every summer of my adolescence there.

The camp was run by Sandy and Eleanor Orr, two charismatic educators who insisted that we adolescents learned how to care about and care for each other, no matter how screwed up we thought we were. Implicitly foreshadowing Sherif's work, they would manufacture crises to create conditions where we had to work together to get through. While wily in, of course, a caring way, they nurtured a generation of offbeat, sometimes genuinely troubled, adolescents who, to this day, feel bound to each other in some deep, umbilical way because of that shared experience. We took trips to Native American pueblos, pack trips on horseback into the mountains, spent days with anthropologists such as John Collier, and worked together during the days to improve the land on which the camp was situated. Making adobe bricks for new construction was a staple, and I can still feel the mud under my feet as I, along with other adolescent city-dwellers, stomped on the clumps of increasingly muddy and malleable earth. I met my first wife, Penny Keith, there, 10 years before we were married.

The glue for this rich and enduring experience, however, was folk music. The music came primarily from counselors and other campers who each summer came to camp with new instruments and newly learned songs to share. Each year guitars, mountain dulcimers, banjos, and autoharps could be heard at any hour of the day when we were not visiting national monuments or making adobe bricks. Howie Mitchell was my mentor. A self-effacing, talented physics and math teacher, Howie was musically as creative as they come, adept playing the dulcimer, guitars, and banjo, and really able to make music out of about anything. Once he made something he called a "doorcimer," a plywood door on which he mounted fret boards and strings to make a quartet of playable dulcimers. His total absorption in ballads of other times and places led me to a depth of appreciation for the social role of folk song. I could visualize the lives of the miners, the love-struck men and women in England or Arkansas, the farmer plowing the field and praying for rain, or the cook on the cattle drive. Howie's gift was to convey a spirit of folk song that preserved its timelessness, its ability to tell a story, and its ability to put you in another life, another time, and another culture.

In addition, folksong served as the foundation of sense of community at the camp. It was what we looked forward to in the evenings, at the ranch or in the many national parks and monuments we visited in our efforts to learn the Native American history of the southwest. Together, we formed a secular choir every summer, and each school year I'd be on the lookout for new material to bring to the following year's experience.

We also learned about the traditional music of the region. Over the years, we came to know individuals from the Taos and Santa Domingo pueblos, and every summer we would be invited to attend festivals or events where Native American traditional music could be heard. In addition, right down the valley was Jenny Wells Vincent, the previous owner of the property on which the camp was located and long-time resident of the San Cristobal valley. Jenny was part of the folk music revival of the 30s and 40s, and, along with other "folkies" of the time, was caught up in the blacklisting of the McCarthy days. She had, for many years, been attempting to preserve local heritage through collecting indigenous songs of the Spanish-speaking communities in New Mexico. When I last saw her a few years ago she was over 80 and still playing accordion and calling square dances in Taos. It is hard to put into words the kinds of effects these experiences and people had on me as a teenager, but I found every summer to be inspirational.

Thus, music became the vehicle we all used to create a sense of community, to develop a shared identity, and, not incidentally, to contribute to the local community through participation in the annual summer fiesta held in Taos. It connected me to the lives and struggles of people led in vastly different ecologies as well as chronicling the celebrations of everyday life. It took an empathic point of view, telling stories through the perspectives of those living them. The appreciation for both the uncommon strengths of common folks and the ways they accommodated to adversity with integrity would all be later incorporated into my hopes for what community psychology could contribute.

I later followed this musical trail to the homes of those whose family traditions had been preserved in song. Through Howie Mitchell, I met George and Gerry Armstrong in Wilmette, Illinois, folk collectors who opened their hearts and home to me for over 30 years until their deaths. Through them, I met and later visited Frank Proffitt, the North Carolina tobacco farmer whose family had, several generations previously, written the song Tom Dooley, later popularized by the Kingston Trio. I still own a mountain dulcimer he made for me in 1964, shortly before his death. I came to know Larry Older who, with his wife Martha, lived in a small house in the Adirondacks. Larry worked on the railroads until he retired, collected antique bottles from the 19th century, and was a source of wonderful songs and stories from his part of the country. When he would play a "bawdy" song, he'd make sure his wife Martha was not in the room to hear it. "Wouldn't be right!," he'd say with a twinkle in his eye. And, finally, I started what would become a 35-year friendship with Sandy and Caroline Paton, for whom I recorded until the mid-1990s. With each I learned about and was accepted into another way of life for which music served as a binding force.

Through these relationships a whole world of the folk music revival opened that I would never have experienced except for the fortuitous events of my adoption, attending St. Albans, and having nothing to do one summer. The folk music community I came to know now spans continents, professions, political stances, urban/rural areas, and ways of life. It includes professional musicians, amateurs who play on the side, appreciators of the music who can't carry a tune, people with record collections of hundreds of 78rpm records from the 1920s and 30s, and others who just simply enjoy getting to know musicians. I learned much from this community, including the adaptive requirements for a folk musician on the road; how to be an unobtrusive house guest, helping with household chores without being asked, and being appreciative of even the most lumpy hide-a-bed. It is a loose but welcoming confederation of people who invite musicians, some of whom are absolute strangers, into their homes for a night or fortnight, who assume the best about you unless you prove otherwise; a network that allows relationships to emerge among what might, from the outside, seem to be "strange bedfellows."

My early formative adolescent folk music years coincided with my high school years at St. Albans, and its educational climate, its clientele, and Ivy League aspirations for its graduates provided a meaningful daily contrast to my blue-collar family and neighborhood context. Overall, I fared pretty well at St. Albans, although I took the "sophomore slump" concept seriously and extended it for my last three high school years, graduating at the very top of the bottom third of my class. Athletics provided a coping cushion; quarterback on the football team, co-captain in basketball, and pitcher on the baseball team.

What seems most relevant to me in retrospect, however, was the kick I got out of being a team player. Whether in sports or music, the concept of being in sync, being in harmony, of developing roles that complemented what others were doing, became an important aspirational goal. So, it was the shared aspects of the culture of team sports and the culture of folk music, those aspects that solidified bonds among participants, that drew me to them; a focus on the song, not the singer. Later in college, I thought about this when I read Fitzgerald's description of Gatsby's smile upon seeing Nick Carraway. It was a smile that "assured you that it had precisely the impression of you that, at your best, you hoped to convey" (Fitzgerald, 1925, p. 48). It saw the best in you and in so doing made the best in you more likely to emerge.

Still, I never transcended my feeling of marginality at St. Albans. As Margaret told me many years later, "we lived on the wrong side of Connecticut Avenue." There were lots of little reminders, such as the first time I went to a friend's house for dinner and found that I had not one but two forks by my plate. We were a one-fork family. As high school progressed, I was increasingly unable to concentrate on studies, felt out of place at school, awkward socially, and could not readily share my experiences with my loving but non-psychologically minded family.

The saving graces for me were adults who took the time to help. Eleanor Orr, from summer camp, was always available for a late night conversation about the meaning of whatever and how I could cope with it. At school Carter Hall, a math teacher, and Dean Stambaugh, an art teacher, took a special interest in my academic and personal survival. They were all critical resources during my academic floundering and existential crisis, providing me with what I would later understand to be emotional support, cognitive guidance, and identity affirmation that whoever I was, I was all right. I sometimes wonder if I would have been as receptive to the influences of these "mentors" if my own family had not understood me better or if I had been better able to start those conversations myself.

While St. Albans by itself provided me with sufficient coping challenges, the contrast between my daily school experience among bright, well-connected whites (primarily) and my local neighborhood culture represented another context to negotiate. In the neighborhood the local playground served as the cultural leveler. It was the singular multicultural site for the neighborhood, where blacks and whites mixed, played with and against each other. On the playground one earned respect the honest way: by being good and knowing how to adapt to the rough but rule-bound playground basketball culture. I acculturated pretty well there. At that point, for a white boy I could jump.

At the time, I was simply coping with quite different experiences in school and the neighborhood. Looking back, however, these contrasting school settings and neighborhood peer groups became the arena to learn first hand about very different cultural, racial, and socioeconomic ways of being. While not all these encounters went smoothly, each elicited and developed different aspects of who and what I would become. While I managed pretty well across these contexts, I never totally identified with or belonged to any of these powerful influences. I was too blue-collar at St. Albans and too St. Albans in my neighborhood. I was fine on the playground, but my playground relationships with black peers did not extend beyond. It was the kind of biculturalism, I later learned, that allows you to adapt behaviorally in multiple contexts while feeling at home in none.

In spite of my lackluster commitment to high school, the education I received at St. Albans was a classical education rich and deep in its influence. Upon graduation, I left for Trinity College in Hartford, Connecticut. Given my academic record, it was only the reputation of St. Albans that persuaded Trinity to take me. Trinity College was a very good fit; a strong school academically with an ongoing folk music community among the students. For two years I majored in both English and Psychology; English because of my love of language and Psychology to further my summer camp interests in how to create a sense of community. English was qualitative ("How do I love thee, let me count the ways"), Psychology quantitative ("How do I love thee: Let me put it on a 9 point scale."). English was aesthetically captivating, Psychology potentially socially useful. While I no longer think that Psychology is necessarily more socially useful than English, I forsook English after two years, taking with me a deep appreciation for language and the life-long friendship of Paul Smith, a Hemingway scholar whose grasp of American literature left indelible impressions about the power of language to convey and to shape experience. I have always aspired to write psychology in such a manner, though with quite variable success.

It was also a time of social turmoil in the country, most visibly in the Civil Rights movement. Issues of civil rights were reflected on campus, and protests, marches, and demonstrations were as much the curriculum as formal courses. And we didn't need to go off campus for issues, as college fraternities at Trinity were functionally segregated. During my freshman year this issue was confronted by a small group of upperclassmen led by a short-haired, energetic Illinois scholar named George Will. Now known for his articulate conservative political perspective and love of the Chicago Cubs, George was then the quite radical editor of Trinity newspaper, the *Tripod*. He and a few others had just resigned from their respective fraternities and banded together to start a new organization open to all. It would be called Q.E.D., from the Latin "Quod Erat Demonstrandum," or "that which was due to be proved," and I enthusiastically became part of it. Itself a marginal organization, the creation of Q. E. D. provided an example of the power of settings to affect, in this case, both members and campus life. It was a wonderful clanjamfrey, representing in some ways the politics of the 1960s and in others the characters in "Revenge of the Nerds," as Q. E. D. always had the highest academic average on campus of extant fraternities.

But folk music was also part of the daily routine. Every Sunday evening the Trinity folksingers would gather together. While, of necessity, we valued enthusiasm over competence, our weekly meetings always ended with anticipation about what new songs the next week would offer. Graduates of that group went on to become anthropologists, engineers, lawyers working in the labor movements of the South as well as in patent law, and legislative aids on Capitol Hill. None of us became full time musicians, but our musical gatherings reflected the zeitgeist of the 1960s into which community psychology was later born. The adaptation of spirituals such as "We Shall Overcome" for the more secular Civil Rights Movement and the traditional ballads from young Joan Baez about the life-threatening hazards of falling in love with someone from a different social class provided a continuity of social issues across cultures and generations. It was here that I met Anne Mayo Muir, and through her, Gordon Bok, two musicians with whom I sang, toured, and recorded for over 25 years.

After college, rather than try my hand at being a full-time musician, I chose graduate school in Clinical Psychology. I had learned a lot about the lives of traveling folk musicians by then and lacked the courage. I also had a passion for psychology, and, under the influence of my professor Curtis Langhorne, decided to attend Ohio State, where he had graduated many years before. It had the best reputation of any school that accepted me, and had a first rate intellectual climate, with both George Kelly and Julian Rotter on the faculty at the time I applied. For my introduction to psychology, George Kelly taught a course in the philosophy of science. Would that more programs did so today. With wit and wisdom, and omitting absolutely none of the 65 items on the reading list, Kelly led us through the early promise and problems of positivism, the logic of inductive and deductive inference, and the philosophical underpinnings of personal construct theory. He would remain an exemplar of intelligence and insightful thinking. His theory of personal constructs, likening the scientific process to that engaged in by each of us in our everyday lives as we try to understand and anticipate our own world, remains a constant reminder of the link between elegant theory and everyday lives. It is precisely this link between theory and everyday lives that I have come to think an ecological perspective in community psychology strives to achieve.

Still, the clinical psychology of the time left precious little room for integrating the social agendas of the 1960s with clinical training, and it was nothing less than a career-defining event when Jim Kelly joined the faculty during my second year. In the midst of developing his ecological analogy, Jim was attempting to define and create a new field he called community psychology. At his intellectual richest, he was pouring out drafts of papers that contained an ecological vision of the world and a profession that would be simultaneously intellectually vibrant, contextually sensitive, and socially engaged. It was worldly, elegant, complex, concerned about social issues, ecological, multilevel, and marginal to the rest of psychology at the time. It was, in short, a perfect person-environment fit for my professional aspirations.

What Kelly taught me over the years is beyond the scope of this effort and was as much by personal example as by intellectual elegance. Jim supervised my Masters and dissertation research, the latter from the University of Michigan, where he moved during my clinical internship year in Colorado. The dissertation was developed during a series of meetings with Jim in the Detroit airport, where, at his suggestion, he'd meet my commuter flight from Columbus and spend several hours discussing first, my dissertation, and, second, this new field emerging from the recent Swampscott Conference called community psychology. Jim's commitment to mentoring and his willingness to go well out of his way for a graduate student were powerful reminders about how to constructively care about the development of others. It was role-modeling at its finest.

By my last year in graduate school, I was, in the imagery of Kuhn (1970), persuaded by but not yet converted to an ecological perspective. Both community psychology and I were still in the formative years, and I did not yet have a clear career path in mind for pursuing this new field. However, Jim was thinking about my future and passed on a letter from a young Stanford-based psychologist named Rudolf Moos seeking postdocs to join him. Rudy, at the time, had conducted a number of studies focusing on topics of great relevance to community psychology, such as how to assess the social context and how to assess person-environment interaction. In collaboration with Peter Houts, he had just published the Ward Atmosphere Scale, the first of what would become many social climate scales. He sent me a number of papers on the generality and specificity of behavior, finding that in real life the main effects were interactions. His focus on people in context and on the context itself seemed like a natural next step, and, with Jim once again providing the opportunity, I accepted the position Rudy subsequently offered.

In the late 1960s, northern California prized itself on being a few years ahead of the rest of the country. Replete with high school student power movements (Berkeley was the role model), the free speech movement, the Black Panther Party to the north, and the omnipresent allure of mind-altering potions, even the psychiatric residents at Stanford were a hip group. The political emphasis on context and social inequality energized my community psychology interest in how institutions, specifically schools, affect the well-being of those in them. This choice of setting also represented as well the confluence of summer camp and high school experiences.

My two years working with Rudy were productive and formative. His preference for data over dogma, his love of pouring over computer printout and making sense of findings, and his passion for getting the work out the door in quality form all took hold in his young protégée. Under Rudy's tutelage, my interest in schools and ecology further consolidated. I developed with him the Classroom Environment Scale (Trickett & Moos, 1973), spending many hours in public schools observing and discussing school with students and teachers. With Frank Ochberg, then a psychiatric resident, I developed a retrospective account of a high school student power movement deftly squashed by a very savvy principal (Ochberg & Trickett, 1970). The principal's commitment to a representative rather than participatory democracy, plus his considerable energy and commitment to build consensus among his colleagues and superiors as events unfolded, resulted in both his survival as principal and the cooling out of the revolutionary fervor of the more radical students. It was an early encounter with the slippery empowerment concept that later became central to community psychology.

The two years in Rudy's laboratory helped consolidate a research career commitment. I learned about the professional life style of the researcher, had days where the singular task was to read and think, and had almost daily conversations with Rudy about data, ideas, and the relation between the two. We planned collaborative work that lasted well beyond my postdoctoral years (e.g., Trickett & Moos, 1974; Moos & Trickett, 1979). In addition, of course, my time and work with him made it possible to be competitive for an academic job at an institution I could not have gotten into as an undergraduate: Yale.

The highlight of my Yale interview was lunch with Seymour Sarason. My only image of him was through his book *Psychology in Community Settings*, written in collaboration with his fellow partisans of the 1960s (Sarason, Levine, Goldenberg, Cherlin, & Bennett, 1966). His informal erudition, excitement about ideas, and elegant and articulate suspicion of the readiness of the psychology of the time to conceptualize and be useful to the world of the future, were heady fare. Seymour shared with folk music the appreciation of history and the ways in which lives reflected time, place, and class. In the final analysis, the opportunity to join him at Yale competed, only briefly, with a lovely offer from Emory Cowen.

We were housed not in the psychology department but in the setting Seymour created to deal with future societies, the Psychoeducational Clinic. Whenever I think of the power of settings, I think of that time and place. Staffed by full time faculty such as Seymour and Dick Reppucci, unforgettable colleagues such as Kate McGraw and Anita Miller, and graduate students such as Rhona Weinstein, Pat O'Neill, Cary Cherniss and, from school psychology, Judie Alpert, we played out weekly the dialectic between thought and action. Each Friday we would meet as a group for several hours to discuss and debate the ideas guiding our work. On a bad day Seymour had more to give than most of us on good days, and his ability to ask questions we would never have thought of and his total support of our efforts sparked an unparalleled integration of passion and reflection. While I learned many things from him during my 8 years at Yale, his admonition about how to spend my time was among the most memorable. Then, as now, the opportunity to become overextended in terms of different projects was an ongoing source of tension, and I would often ask Seymour for his advice. "Ed," he said, "the only criterion for you is whether or not you will learn something from doing it. If you don't think you're going to, don't do it."

Other colleagues and experiences at Yale also reinforced my appreciation of the power of settings to nurture and sustain. With Bill Hawley from Education, John McConahay from Psychology, and Judy Gruber, then a graduate student in Political Science, I began a study of the creation and evolution of High School in the Community, an alternative public inner city high school begun in response to the race riots of the previous decade (Trickett, 1991). High School in the Community was the ultimate exploration of how teachers turned the idea of empowerment into the social structure of a school, a question of central importance to all of us trying to understand how to integrate thought with action. I followed the school over a 14-year period and saw how a combination of committed and creative teachers, powerful ideas, and responsive and reflective social structures could combine to make a school work for students, parents, and teachers (Trickett, 1991). I kept in touch with the school's founders, doing a benefit concert for them in the 1980s and, in 1983, was asked to deliver their commencement address. It was the summer camp of my youth relocated in urban New Haven; the kind of setting that Sarason envisioned when nominating sense of community as the goal by which community interventions should be judged.

There was, of course, life beyond Yale. During these years, daughters Jennifer and Kate were born at Yale-New Haven hospital, and I continued my involvement in the flourishing folk music scene in New England. In the mid-1970s, I began what would be a 26-year musical collaboration with Ann Mayo Muir and Gordon Bok. Beginning in 1974, we spent about a month a year together, half the time practicing 6-10 hours a day and the other few weeks trying to convince audiences that the practicing was worth it. When we decided to call it quits three years ago we had amassed thousands of miles on the road, discovered many "hide-a-bed and breakfasts" at caring souls' houses, developed many friends, and produced two handfuls of CDs. My association with them cemented in my mind the synthesis of folk music, with its articulation of the lives of people in struggle, whether it be with politicians, racism, or the sea, and a community psychology that focused on understanding those lives and giving them voice. But the sense of community emerging from a good concert was probably the best.

For my 8 years at Yale, I professed during the week and was often on the road as a folk musician on the weekends, with Gordon and Ann and on my own. While exhausting, the music part of my life recaptured the freedom and excitement of travel that I had first experienced with the Washington Cathedral Choir and later traveling to camp in New Mexico in school busses. But the integration of these two lives was sometimes complicated. For example, within the first week I landed in New Haven to begin my teaching career at Yale, I left to go to Woodstock at the request of Rosalie Sorrels, who said her manager (also Dylan's manager at the time) could get her onto a minor stage there. Dave Bromberg and I would be her "band." We stayed there for several days, finally getting flown down to the site by helicopter at dawn. We never did play on stage, but I had some conversations backstage about my instrument, the hammered dulcimer, with John Sebastian and Jerry Garcia. However, it wasn't easy explaining the experience to my newly found colleagues at Yale, whose reaction left me feeling as much like a curiosity as an assistant professor. And one Friday in Ithaca, New York, I did a colloquium for the Cornell Psychology Department in the afternoon and a concert for the Cornell Folksong Society that night.

While I have been asked both "how do you do it" and "why do you do it," I have come to see my involvement in these contrasting worlds as providing a life-long experience bound together by sense of community and common cause. I have benefited immensely from immersion in both "cultures," although I have generally alternated between them, keeping them in relatively distinct compartments, rather than integrating them. The main exception is probably the folk music concert I did at the first Division 27 biennial in South Carolina in 1987, a program of folk music that I hoped would illustrate the connection between community psychology and folk music through a focus on lives of struggle, love, and hope lived in contrasting sociocultural contexts. While I enjoyed putting that concert together, the stress I experienced performing folk music in front of a community psychology audience was far more than I anticipated. I felt patently outside of both the folk music and community psychology cultures in that context.

The language of "culture" is one that I subsequently explored at my next position at the University of Maryland. Maryland had begun a fascinating social experiment in clinical/community psychology begun almost a decade previously by Forrest Tyler. Forrest was intent on integrating clinical and community psychology through a dual commitment to cultural diversity and empowerment. The program reflected Forrest's deep commitment to ethnic minority student admission and retention, and issues of race and social justice permeated discussions about the curriculum, faculty hiring and student admissions, research topics, and, most pervasively, the social climate of the program.

The power of this setting and its social climate exerted an enduring influence on my thinking about community psychology as well as my own role in the field, as it was during these years that the ecology of diversity became my research agenda. The scholarly highlight of these years was the opportunity to develop with Rod Watts and Dina Birman a conference that would later become *Human Diversity: Perspectives of People in Context* (Trickett, Watts, & Birman, 1994). It crystallized an overarching agenda around the integration of culture and context as a community psychology agenda, and aided in developing a network of diverse psychologists committed to issues of diversity that remains. In addition, Maryland provided the opportunity of both teaching and learning from a diverse group of graduate students around issues of multiculturalism in public schools. Forrest's insistence on welcoming into the training environment people who themselves represent multiple ethnicities, countries, religions, and sexual orientations provided a living example of both the complexities and promise of what we can learn through encounters with diversity. Our own stumblings, however, sometimes vindicated Walt Kelly's social commentary, articulated through Pogo, that "we has met the enemy and it is us."

Today, from my vantage point at the University of Illinois at Chicago, the same themes that were reflected and developed over time center my professional and personal life. The integration of ecology and diversity has centered on issues facing immigrant and refugee populations. Dina and I continue to collaborate on a project she initiated with the Maryland Office for New Americans in 1998 on the adolescent-family-school relationship in Soviet Jewish, and, later, Vietnamese and Somali communities in Maryland (Birman & Trickett, 2001; Birman, Trickett, & Vinokurov, 2002). This work is now shifting to Chicago, where we are learning about refugee communities through evaluating public school initiatives to educate and acculturate these youth and agency programs that provide much-needed services. This project reflects my hope for and participation in a future of community psychology that focuses on the contexts of diversity and the diversity of contexts. As usual, my involvement in this work has been as an outsider; an American in refugee communities and a white person in communities of color. However, this involvement has been optional rather than one borne of necessity and one which has been a heuristic for intercultural collaboration as well as an increased appreciation of what privileges I have and what others have who are very different from me. I am fortunate to work with fascinating people in both university and community attempting to learn about and influence the life chances of relatively voiceless groups new to the country. And, of course, the pot luck dinners include food from all over the world.

A recurrent source of learning, however, has been the opportunity to link collaborative relationships across cultures with opportunities to connect with and learn from different segments of multicultural communities. When I worked with the former Soviet community in collaboration with Dina and my dear colleague Andrey Vinokurov, then a graduate student, we each were differentially able to connect more quickly and trustingly with varied constituencies in the Soviet community and the school serving their children; Dina with parents and former Soviet adolescent young women, Andrey with former Soviet young men, particularly those in trouble in the school, and me with the establishment folks in the school context, including the PTA. The connections were affected by both differences in personal style and well as those associated with age, gender, Russian language fluency, and culture of origin. However, we soon understood that the three of us had access to different information as diverse players shared their thoughts with each of us differently. Through this process we learned the extent to which aspects of our own cultural frameworks were both unarticulated and divergent, and we worked hard to create a self-reflective process that could enrich what we were learning.

For example, one of the recurrent themes we heard form Soviet adolescents about differences between their previous life and life here in the U.S. involved friendship. The Soviet perception was that friendship here reflects a shallow, quixotic sense of commitment, a "here one day gone the next" transience that makes relationships suspect; not like the deep, rich, dependable, stick-up-for-your-friend-at-any-cost sense of friendship they experienced in the former Soviet Union. Dina and Andrey immediately understood what they meant; it resonated with them at the deep level on which culture operates. I didn't really get it until I heard the story about a book-throwing incident in one of the classes. A Soviet student had thrown a book at an American student while the teacher's back was turned. He missed his target, but the teacher saw that something was going on, and asked who did it. After a moment of uncomfortable silence, an American student pointed to the Soviet student as the perpetrator. The teacher told the student to go to the Vice-Principal's office and, when he got up to leave, all the other Soviet students in the class got up and left with him. That's what they meant by friendship.

Such events represent what my anthropology colleague Mike Agar (1996) calls "rich points," those moments when the awareness of differential perception or understanding between people becomes acknowledged and serves as a resource for mutual learning about the world view of the other and the world view of the self. Searching for such rich points seems useful in the community psychology dialogue about the contexts of diversity and the diversity of contexts.

REFERENCES

Agar, M. (1996). *The Professional Stranger*, 2nd Edition. San Diego: Academic Press.

Birman, D., & Trickett, E. J. (2001). The Process of Acculturation in First Generation Immigrants: A Study of Soviet Jewish Refugee Adolescents and Parents. *Journal of Cross-Cultural Psychology*, 32(4), 456-477.

Birman, D., Trickett, E. J., & Vinokurov, A. (2002). Acculturation and Adaptation of Soviet Jewish Refugee Adolescents: Predictors of Adjustment Across Life Domains. *American Journal of Community Psychology*.

Fitzgerald, F. S. (1925). *The Great Gatsby*. New York. Charles Scribner's Sons.

Kuhn, T. H. (1970). *The Structure of Scientific Revolutions*. Chicago: University of Chicago Press.

Moos, R.H., & Trickett, E.J. (1979). Determinants of Classroom Environments. In Moos, R.H., *Evaluating Educational Environments*. San Francisco: Jossey-Bass, pp. 159-182.

Ochberg, F.M., & Trickett, E.J. (1970), Administrative responses to racial tensions in a high school. *Community Mental Health Journal*, 6, 470-483.

Sarason, S.B., Levine, M., Goldenberg, I.I., Cherlin, D., & Bennett, E. (1966). *Psychology in Community Settings*. New York: John Wiley and Sons.

Trickett, E.J. (1991). *Living an Idea: Empowerment and the Evolution of an Alternative High School*. Brookline, MA: Brookline Books.

Trickett, E.J., & Moos, R.H. (1973). Assessment of the Psychosocial Environment of the High School Classroom. *Journal of Educational Psychology*, 65, 1, 93-102.

Trickett, E.J., & Moos, R.H. (1974). Personal Correlates of Contrasting Environments: Student Satisfactions in High School Classrooms. *American Journal of Community Psychology*, 2, 1-12. Reprinted in O'Leary, K.D., & O'Leary, S.G. (Eds.), *Classroom Management: The Successful Use of Behavior Modification*, 2nd edition. Pergamon Press.

Trickett, E.J., Watts, R., & Birman, D. (Eds.) (1994). *Human Diversity: Perspectives on People in Context*. San Francisco: Jossey Bass.

The Making of a Community Psychologist: Naïve Idealism, Supportive Contexts and Good Fortune

Jean Ann Linney

University of South Carolina

SUMMARY. Childhood and young adult experiences during an era of significant social change are described as cultivating a personal worldview concerned with social justice and the importance of social context at the individual and collective levels. Parental support and expectations for excellence in achievement, religious beliefs grounded in personal and social responsibility, and early recognition of inequities in opportunity and resources combined to form a value base consistent with the emerging field of community psychology. Some non-traditional gender socialization propelled motivation and provided inoculation against subsequent discrimination and harassment. Strong mentoring and supportive education and work settings solidified identity as an ecologically minded, action-oriented community psychologist. *[Article copies available for a fee from The Haworth Document Delivery Service: 1-800-HAWORTH. E-mail address: <docdelivery@haworthpress.com> Website: <http://www.HaworthPress.com> © 2004 by The Haworth Press, Inc. All rights reserved.]*

KEYWORDS. Community psychology, social context, women psychologists, gender stereotypes, narratives, professional identity

---

Address correspondence to: Jean Ann Linney, Department of Psychology, University of South Carolina, Columbia, SC 29208-0182 (E-mail: LINNEY@SC.EDU).

[Haworth co-indexing entry note]: "The Making of a Community Psychologist: Naïve Idealism, Supportive Contexts and Good Fortune." Linney, Jean Ann. Co-published simultaneously in *Journal of Prevention & Intervention in the Community* (The Haworth Press, Inc.) Vol. 28, No. 1/2, 2004, pp. 81-102; and: *Six Community Psychologists Tell Their Stories: History, Contexts, and Narrative* (eds: James G. Kelly, and Anna V. Song) The Haworth Press, Inc., 2004, pp. 81-102. Single or multiple copies of this article are available for a fee from The Haworth Document Delivery Service [1-800-HAWORTH, 9:00 a.m. - 5:00 p.m. (EST). E-mail address: docdelivery@haworthpress.com].

http://www.haworthpress.com/web/JPIC
© 2004 by The Haworth Press, Inc. All rights reserved.
Digital Object Identifier: 10.1300/J005v28n01_05

Community psychology was an emerging field when I began thinking about graduate school. There were just a handful of programs in community psychology. As an undergraduate psychology major I'd not heard of this specialty area or even the concept. In many ways it was a fortunate accident that I entered the clinical psychology program at the University of Illinois at Urbana-Champaign in 1972. This decision and a number of paths followed since then were the result of choices that sometimes reflected taking the comfortable path of least resistance (e.g., going to graduate school), while other choice points were based on what felt like the right thing to do at the time (e.g., job changes). Like many women of my generation, my professional life and pathways weren't envisioned beforehand. My lifeline wasn't as planned as it might appear in hindsight because like most women my age I grew up with few realistic career options outside of wife and mother.

My personal and professional lives have been quite positive, and because of that I've often been asked what stimulated my interest in community psychology. I grew up in a hard working, stable, middle class family in the New York suburban area. In many ways my family life and childhood hopes were quite stereotypic of the 1950s, breadwinner father, stay-at-home mother, four children and a dog. I hoped to grow up to be a mother like Donna Reed in her television show. Although I was an adolescent in the 1960s, the political and social movements of that time were not much a part of my consciousness, and in some ways were events that perhaps I should be embarrassed to say, I hardly paid attention to until I was in college and political action broke out on our campus. A number of childhood experiences highlighted a state of affairs in the world that seemed inherently unfair to me and I have vivid memories of being troubled by these experiences, questioning where these practices came from and why they continued. Many of these experiences probably had direct and indirect influences on my subsequent development as a community psychologist.

FORMATIVE VALUES AND IDEALS: THE PERSONAL CONTEXT

Family Context

My parents emphasized hard work, high expectations, and doing the best you can in whatever you do. There was a strong value for respect, responsibility and reciprocity, perhaps the early roots of my systems orientation.

I'm the oldest of four children (two sisters and a brother). Each of us has taken different pathways into adulthood. I'm the only one who moved away from the northeast, the only Democrat, one of only two with a college degree. Both of my parents are college graduates, my mother a math major, my father a chemistry major. My mother worked in her father's company and later for an auditing firm until I was born. As far as I know she hasn't had a paying job since then. My father had hopes of going to medical school, but instead took a job in pharmaceutical sales when he graduated from college following military service in World War II. He retired from that company 38 years later as a senior executive in the corporate headquarters. In many ways he is an exemplar of the American success story. He worked hard, always brought office work home and frequently went to his office on Saturday mornings. He wanted a better life for himself and his family and was successful in achieving that.

My father's parents were Irish immigrants, poor and proud, although I never knew them. My mother's parents were at least second generation Americans, with a German surname. I never knew much about my mother's family history. She always told us we were Americans and that talk about family roots in any other country was silly. At least in this area, attention was not focused on past accomplishments (or sins), but rather on what you have and what you do with it. Through my maternal grandparents I got a glimpse of the lifestyle of the upper class. My maternal grandfather had a successful warehouse and moving company in New York City specializing in moving large pieces of sculpture, art, and pianos. His customers included the Vanderbilts, the Carnegies, the Rockefellers and other wealthy families in New York. My grandparents had a summer home at the beach. Two or three times my grandmother took me to Broadway shows with lunch at the Waldorf Astoria in New York City. Despite my grandfather's death when I was 7 years old, I remember him in many different contexts. He is always described as a stern man who believed that children should be seen and not heard, but he drove me to school every day for the year that we lived with them. He patiently waited if I was late, he surreptitiously gave me a nickel every school day to buy ice cream in the cafeteria. I could tell that he was proud of me, my good grades and good manners.

Education was highly valued in our family, in part because it was a vehicle to a better life, but perhaps more because it insured independence and the flexibility afforded by financial means. I was always a good student (except first year in college). I liked school. I liked to "play school" with friends when I was in the elementary grades. My mother taught me to read even before I went to kindergarten. My parents always communicated the importance of doing your best, not only in school, but whatever you took on. I remember instances of bringing home a report card with all A's, and my father saying that was pretty good, but maybe next time I could get some A+s. His affect communicated congratulations and pride, as well as expectation for continuing sustained effort and perhaps higher expectations–a balance that was motivating without engendering helplessness or defeat.

My parents are Republicans, identifying with the rugged individualism ideology of that party. Having worked hard to succeed even in the face of some discrimination, they tend to minimize the value of collective action, endorse accommodation and melting pot notions of diversity, and believe in both free market, capitalist market models and survival of the fittest. We didn't talk much about politics or current events at home when I was growing up, but I do remember feeling uneasy with some of the political commentary at the dinner table. Racial integration for example, seemed to be something they worried about but I couldn't understand why. One salient incident that highlighted race and class for me happened in third grade. I wanted to get together after school with the girl who sat next to me in school. I asked if she could walk home with me to play after school, then my mother could drive her home. She lived in an apartment complex 5 or 6 miles from our house, but we had catechism classes (religious education) in her neighborhood once a week, so I knew where it was. My mother told me that wouldn't work out. I asked if we could do this on the day of catechism, since that wouldn't be an extra trip, or if I could take the bus home with her on a day that I had catechism and just stay until time for class. There was some reason why each of these wouldn't work. After much thought, brainstorming, and some frustration, it occurred to me that maybe I wasn't going to be allowed to do this because my friend was "a colored girl" and she lived in what today would be known as a public housing project. This was 1959 and despite our prominent collective memories, racial segregation was not limited to the deep south. These attitudes were part of that social time and were not effectively challenged until a decade later. I never went to my friend's house and she never came to mine, but we played together at school. School provided a venue to transcend hurtful social conventions. Nearly all of my professional life I've viewed schools as an important context for the work of community psychology and a place that could foster competent, healthy development.

Overall, there was little discussion and certainly no disagreement with my parents' decisions or opinions. I remember numerous instances in which my perspective was quite different from one or both of my parents, but I understood that there was little to be gained by disagreeing or arguing. I was just a kid. My coping strategy was patience and time. I was very confident that once I was a "grown-up" I could say and do as I wanted and believed, and so I looked toward that future. My early experiences with inter-racial friendships and polite but powerfully limiting attitudes were probably not insignificant in shaping my later research activity on the effects of school desegregation, racial attitudes and understanding cultural and ethnic differences and my investment in mentoring non-white students.

Religious Education and an Agenda for Social Justice

Catholic nuns in particular and religious education in general have been very important influences in my life. A great deal has been written about the negative effects of Catholic training and the actions of the nuns–their use of rulers, critically demanding attitudes, expectations for unquestioning obedience and the like. For me these are not salient memories, nor descriptive of my experience. Instead, the nuns I saw in weekly religious education class, and later in Catholic high school were important role models of powerful, effectual women who devoted their lives to bettering the circumstances of others. To this day, the best teacher I've ever had was a nun. She taught medieval literature and the history of the English language. I've never been so much in awe of a teacher's expertise and command of the subject matter, and her ability to bring it to life for a group of students. Sister Lorraine was pursuing a graduate degree weekends on top of her full time teaching position, advising the student newspaper, and working a soup kitchen for poor people in the neighborhood. It appeared to me that she pursued an enviable level of excellence and selflessness in everything she did. She had a calmness and sense of security about her that spread to others. She connected the events of centuries ago to our contemporary lives, taught us about the continuity and ubiquity of human struggles, and the strength and sustenance that could be derived from the pursuit of moral causes.

As early as first grade I remember going to weekly catechism class always taught by nuns. These women were strong, caring leaders in my eyes. Early in elementary school I began thinking about becoming a nun and in high school seriously considered entering the novitiate. What attracted me to this vocation was not the religious life per se, but the opportunity for commitment and dedication to social justice goals and the collective good. Certainly in the first half of the decade of the 1960's there were few models of these types of activities for women. Interestingly my mother and friends reacted quite negatively to my talk of becoming a nun, and I postponed any action.

I was enrolled in Catholic school at the beginning of seventh grade and continued through high school. The teachings and practices of the Catholic Church were a fertile foundation for community psychology, and I was well schooled. These teachings focus attention on giving of one's time, talent and treasure for others, especially those in need. The Catholic Church is defined as the collective of its members and the strength of the church is dependent on the connections and collective actions of the members toward improving quality of life for others. The teachings of the Catholic Church place a high premium on good works. Christ says "whatever you do for the least of my brethren you do for me." There is considerable attention to sacrifice, delay of gratification, and the prospect that one's action may not really change the situation, but there is value in the process and the effort.

The Catholic Church is often characterized, and criticized, as a hierarchical, gendered, discriminatory organization that stifles intellectual freedom. You may be wondering how this context would contribute to the development of a community psychologist. While at some meta level, the negative stereotypes may be accurate, the local life of the Catholic church is quite participatory, governed by an elected parish council. Although women are still not eligible to become priests, women are important decision-makers in the activities of the local parish and the regional dioceses. Issues of church doctrine are still decided exclusively by the pope from Rome and the Catholic Church has consistently held a position that protects life, supporting a prohibition on birth control, abortion and the death penalty. At the same time, many active Catholics hold personal views that are different from these.

Despite what may seem like total engagement and commitment to the Catholic Church, I remember being skeptical in childhood, and some of this skepticism was the early foundation for concerns about fairness, justice, and the role of context. For example, early on I was taught that only those who were baptized could go to heaven. This not only bothered me, but seemed horribly unfair. I was born into a Christian family and subsequently baptized without my knowledge. It seemed to me that one's family was some type of accident, and I couldn't believe that any god would deprive an innocent child of eternal happiness because her parents didn't have her baptized! This kind of thinking is one of the earlier instances of my growing awareness of the realities of differential resources and opportunities afforded to each of us and the cascading effect on subsequent opportunities and life trajectories.

Gender Stereotypes Counterbalanced

Achievement expectations were not gender specific in my family. My father taught me to throw a baseball, expected me to help him with yardwork, and taught each of us to control and channel our emotions. My mother regularly refuted the gendered schemas I was acquiring from experience and observation. She frequently told her daughters not to rush into marriage. "You're a long time married" she would say. Get an education, live on your own, travel and have your own money before marriage was her advice. She also planted seeds regarding career goals that challenged prevailing gender roles. Around age 5, I told someone I wanted to be a nurse. "Why not be a doctor?" my mother asked. Later in high school I talked about being an elementary school teacher, and my mother suggested I become a high school or college teacher. When I expressed reservation that I wasn't capable of doing these, she always said something like, "of course you can. You can be anything you want to be." These were important messages, repeated and reinforced that I don't believe most of my friends were hearing from their mothers or fathers.

Reality told me that my mother's missive wasn't really true, however, and I came to be annoyed at the ways in which rules, policies and practices precluded girls from ever accomplishing certain things. For example, I wanted to be president of my high school class, but the nomination and ballot construction process was structured in such a way that a girl would never even appear on the ballot for president. The process involved all members of the class submitting written nominations for class officers. Teachers counted the nominations and the two *boys* with the highest number of nominations ran for president, the two girls with the highest number of nominations ran for vice-president, regardless of the absolute number of nominations received. You won't be surprised to know that the next two boys ran for treasurer, and the next two girls ran for secretary. This was not a policy that students were privy to, but as a senior I was a member of the Student Council and participated in the counting of nominations learning this hidden rule that insured a male was always elected the leader.

When I was looking to make application to college, gendered practices were salient. As Irish Catholics, the University of Notre Dame was always on the radar screen in our household. In 1968 females were not considered for admission. Because I was a woman, applications to Georgetown, Princeton, Yale, the University of Virginia and dozens of other prestigious colleges would not be considered. At the time I remember being frustrated by this state of affairs, feeling it was unfair, but not knowing quite what could be done to change the situation.

I ended up attending a small liberal arts college that to this day is a confederation of a men's college and a women's college. There is one faculty, one curriculum, coed classes, but distinct areas of campus identified with each school, separate student governments and student affairs divisions. We experienced the best of the single gender institution in terms of leadership, power and mutual support, along with the integrative challenges of the co-ed setting. It was at this college that politics, social justice, personal courage, political action and social change became salient, and my interest in psychology was kindled.

Initially I had no interest in attending Hobart and William Smith Colleges. My parents went there, it was small, in the middle of nowhere, and few people have ever heard of the school. But it turned out I was not accepted at the other two schools where I applied. While this was one of the most humbling and humiliating experiences of my life (I graduated second in my high school class and expected to be accepted wherever I applied), it was fortunate for me that I enrolled. The experience of rejection, or perhaps the reality check about my relationship to the larger world, had important implications for other parts of my life as well. College provided more than an academic education for me; it was an opportunity to be involved in modest change initiatives and to formulate a personal agenda for attending to my social justice concerns.

INTELLECTUAL AND EDUCATIONAL CONTEXT: FINDING PATHWAYS

The first session of orientation at college was prototypic of my overall experience there. Expecting tours of the campus and the opportunity to get my library card, I was shocked when we reported to the assigned room and a student leader asked a small group of us, "Who here believes in God?" That question was followed by individual questioning about why or why not, what evidence we had, and how this affected our day-to-day lives. The four years I spent in college presented a series of similar challenges to think about issues and to have a position that could be explained and defended. The expectation that each of us had a responsibility to make a difference during our lives, to contribute in some way that would leave the world a better place was repeatedly reinforced.

A great deal changed in both my immediate community and the larger world during the time I was in college. During my first year, women students had curfews, housemothers in the dorms, and were not admitted to the dining hall unless wearing a skirt. We were required to sign in and out of the dormitory each time we left and returned to the building. We nervously gathered for the annual birthday lottery for the military draft and helped male friends pursue conscientious objector status or flee to Canada if some other deferment from service in Vietnam wasn't available.

This was an incredible time to be a college student. Political issues became very personal as friends faced the draft and forced military service, and family connections were likely to determine one's fate. Antiwar activity, civil rights initiatives and the right to abortion were daily, in-your-face occurrences. It was not unusual to have to walk through a campus demonstration or protest to get to class. You couldn't avoid thinking about your own position on many of these issues because the effects were in front of you more often than not, whether it was supporting a boycott of grapes in the cafeteria, being asked to sign a petition, or learning that a student in your dorm had thrown a pipe bomb into the ROTC offices. For much of my time in college I was among the more conservative people I knew, despite maintaining a network of friends that spanned the political spectrum.

Students on my campus learned first hand about the effectiveness of community organizing efforts, the limits of the law in protecting both the status quo and those seeking change, and the possibility of deadly consequences to peaceful actions when students died at Kent State University. We also accomplished significant local change in college practices through rational, data driven, logical arguments, negotiation, and collective action.

By my fourth year of college much had changed. Curfews were gone, skirts were rarely seen in the dining hall, and sign-ins were limited to once in a 48 hour period no longer requiring the detailed information about where and with whom we were going. The draft had been eliminated, Watergate was the subject of daily conversations, and *Roe v. Wade* was decided. I had witnessed and participated in significant change in my immediate environment that resulted from collective action, dialogue, and planned initiatives.

Application to graduate school was a means to the end of establishing my own independence and autonomy. After several years in college I was certain that I didn't want to live at my parents' home following graduation. Going on to graduate school would be easily accepted by my parents, avoiding a confrontation with them about where I would live (since I didn't have plans to marry). I applied to graduate schools distant from my home, thinking that this would insure opportunity to establish independence. Having been in a small college, my understanding of psychology as a discipline was more integrative than the reality of the field. I applied to graduate programs in clinical, because I thought that was the route to application of psychology. I had also received considerable reinforcement from friends for my abilities as a counselor and confidante, and so becoming some type of therapist seemed reasonable also. My post graduate degree image included a split-level home, husband and kids, part time therapy practice in the lower level of the house, and part time, probably pro bono work at a mental health clinic or community action center.

Determined not to repeat my earlier college application process and risk not being accepted, I applied to 16 graduate programs heavily weighted in the direction of weaker schools. The application to the University of Illinois was precipitated by one of my faculty references who had seen my GRE scores. He felt I should be applying to better places and refused to send letters until I selected at least one school from the top 20 list he had given me. I was certain that this would be a wasted application along with the associated fees, so I selected the school with the lowest application fee–University of Illinois at Urbana-Champaign–seeking to minimize my losses. I was also intrigued by this department because it had a PsyD track. I had serious reservations about my ability to complete a research dissertation, but I also knew that on the off chance that I got accepted, I wouldn't be able to turn down the chance to attend a top flight program. The PsyD program looked like an interesting option because I understood it to mean that the students didn't do a dissertation, and that sounded good to me.

I was offered admission to the doctoral program at Illinois and accepted with excitement and trepidation. (I had applied for the PsyD program but, as it turned out, the first year curriculum was no different from that for the PhD program and I quickly lost interest in the psychotherapy components of the training, opting for the PhD track.) My first year of graduate school was very stressful, both in terms of the amount of time it took me to complete assignments and my perception of my own abilities and interests relative to my classmates. It was typical for me to come to class, listen to the early part of the class discussion and think that I had read the wrong articles because what I gleaned from the assigned readings was so different from those who held the floor of discussion. Midway through the first semester I was beginning to think that I wouldn't make it through the program, but nearly panicked at the prospects of what I would do instead. Fortunately I found a classmate with similar intellectual perspectives and we became close friends and confidantes.

My reactions to many of the readings and discussions in my courses highlighted for me my tendency to see contextual explanations first, and person explanations later across a variety of topical areas. When we talked about treatment (this was a clinical program after all), I was thinking early identification, early intervention and prevention. As an undergraduate I had initiated a companionship therapy program at a state hospital not too far from the college. At its peak we had 50 students visiting chronic backward patients once a week. I was visiting the hospital at least two days a week to visit my own patient and oversee the program. I observed phenomenal changes in the patients we spent time with, not unlike much of the early research on non-professional helpers. Despite dramatic gains in daily functioning, I never had confidence that any of these patients would return to the community or could even survive outside the hospital having become victims of institutionalization. Many days as I left the hospital and drove down the long driveway to the highway I passed an ambulance bringing someone to the admissions unit. This experience solidified my belief that we had to figure out a way to keep people from ever having to enter these kinds of places, hence my interest in prevention and the development of alternative models of service delivery.

My experience as a residence hall advisor (RA) in my college's first co-ed dormitory was also important in shaping my perspectives on mental health service delivery models. My floor had about 80 men and women, with rooms alternating by sex. In many ways the collection of students in the dorm presented some unique problems including students who hoped their social life would improve with daily proximity to potential intimate partners, and others who planned to use this context as a way to cohabitate. There were several students on my floor who were using heavy-duty drugs, drinking too much alcohol, or involved in other self defeating behaviors. Since my academic advisor was the clinical psychologist and director of the campus counseling center, I often talked with him about these students (without mentioning names) and asked his advice about how I could be helpful as their RA. From this experience I discovered the potential of consultation models both in terms of enhancing my capacity as the RA and in initiating some low-level interventions that often had beneficial effects.

Both the experiences at the state hospital and in the dorm fueled my interests in the need for alternative models of mental health service delivery, the primary focus of the personal statement that accompanied my graduate school applications. This orientation came with me to graduate school and without question affected my interpretation and understanding of the readings and discourse I was exposed to early in graduate school.

Experiencing Gender as a Detriment

The first year in graduate school the negative effect of gender on performance evaluation and opportunity became personal. Gender seemed to be affecting the evaluation of the women in my class, and in turn our grades. I received early feedback that my participation in class was weak, and participation was about a third of the course grades. I knew this feedback was accurate and I worked to increase my participation. Using standard behavioral techniques, I set goals for contributing comments in each class and charted my progress. I increased my participation substantially, yet the next feedback from faculty was no different than the first! I concluded that what I was saying must be of little consequence, so I tried some different strategies to increase the value, importance and significance of my contributions–still no change in feedback. Being high on the self disclosure dimension, I mentioned this while having lunch with three other women from my class. They had received the same feedback. I found this hard to believe because one of these women was, in my opinion, the most vocal member of the class and was certainly intellectually intimidating to me. As we talked, we decided to collect data. We charted the verbal activity of everyone in the class and asked several of the men about their evaluative feedback regarding class participation. We found that in terms of behavior counts, the women were contributing as much or more than the men in the class. None of the men we asked had been told their participation was low, but we also learned about numerous out-of-class settings where the male students interacted with male faculty (there were no female faculty in the program at the time), e.g., handball matches, poker night, intramural football and baseball games, and the not-so-occasional beer after class. Not only did the women not participate in these activities, I certainly didn't know about them, and it was socially awkward for us as single women to initiate these interactions with the married male faculty. We decided to ask for a meeting with a handful of the core faculty teaching the first year courses to discuss the situation. Armed with data, we presented our concerns about how our grades and overall assessment were being affected, and the potential consequences of this for our future careers. The faculty listened and asked for suggestions. I subsequently learned to play poker and regularly attended the football and baseball games, going with the team for a drink after the game. Playing poker was hard because I had absolutely no interest in this game, but I've been a sports fan most of my life, had a friend playing in the NFL and enjoyed being an involved spectator at these events. I became a regular at the various games and post game activities, and when I passed my comprehensive exam, I was given my own team jersey.

In my first job, I experienced different forms of sexual harassment and felt that I was being treated as unable to take care of myself, not a peer among the faculty. The sexual harassment took different forms, the most obnoxious of which was having to deal with a colleague who appeared naked during work-related interchanges. Neither the department chair nor the dean of the college were responsive to my complaints and requests for intervention, and at that time there was no legal recourse to pursue. This situation, in combination with the patronizing environment of the department, was something that I'd not experienced before. My response was to go on the job market again, believing that I had simply gotten myself into an environment that wasn't productive for me.

Fortunately my second job post graduate school afforded considerable validation for my ideas and skills, strong mentoring from my area head (Dick Reppucci) and one of the senior women in the department (Mavis Hetherington). There was encouragement to combine family with career, although some of the suggested strategies for accomplishing this were not within my reach (e.g., hire a live-in nanny to take care of the house and children). I married in the second year of this academic position and have always had unconditional support from my husband for my career choices and strong encouragement to advance. He had some graduate work in psychology when we married, and subsequently finished a PhD in psychology. He has worked in both university and human service agency settings. We have successfully integrated marriage, children and career for nearly 25 years now.

Mentors and Flexible Structures

Throughout graduate school I was fortunate to have been part of a fantastic action research team with a wonderful set of mentors. Late in my first year, I realized I might be left without an assistantship for my second year or worse, assigned to something that I wasn't interested in doing. I approached Ed Seidman and asked if he and Julian Rappaport would hire me as a research assistant on their grant. I liked many of the graduate students working on that project, and despite the fact that I got nervous and very self conscious around Julian, working with them looked like a good option for the second year. At the time I had no idea what a great move this assertive request was to be, especially since it was motivated more by the people on the project than the substance of the research activity. I started working on the Educational Pyramid project in the elementary school intervention strand the summer after my first year and continued with this project until I left Illinois for my first job.

At the first research team meeting I was assigned to carry out a factor analysis on a data set for a new measure. I had barely made it through the required core sequence in statistics and had no idea how to do a factor analysis. Doing my best to control my anxiety, I asked for some pointers on how to approach this task. A week and many hours at the computing center later, I came back with a printout.

Despite this nerve wracking beginning, the three years working on this project were great. Both Ed and Julian allowed me to take on leadership roles supervising the school-based project and eventually supervising all four projects of the grant. They asked for my ideas and incorporated them into the research. They clearly conveyed expectations that I should figure out how to do whatever needed to be done, affirmed their confidence in my abilities, provided informational support, and delivered those messages with a bit of humor. Our interactions engendered enough confidence to minimize avoidance of the tasks but maintained performance expectations that resulted in quite a lot of time devoted to task accomplishment. The mentoring relationship was affirming and collegial. Every day I felt engaged and challenged by how to study what was happening in the schools, where to find models to understand it, and how to translate these into effective change efforts. It was hard. It was energizing. It was fun. Nearly thirty years later I still look forward to getting together with folks from these projects, and I'm still immersed in questions of how to study individual-setting processes and effect change.

Scientific and Intellectual Context

As I recall, the big controversies in psychology during my graduate school years involved the ethical conduct of research, the limitations of experimental laboratory paradigms, ecological validity, moving toward multivariable transactional considerations, and the limits of behaviorism. Across the country the courts were deciding cases on the implementation of school desegregation and the rights of children. Communities were dealing with the implications of these decisions. The use of intelligence tests for placement decisions and the limits of state assigned stigma resulting from enrollment in special education classes were also being played out in the courts. I was particularly aware of community reactions to school busing for desegregation because the school district collaborating with our grant project was court ordered to desegregate. Everyone was on edge about how this would be accomplished. Their desegregation ultimately became the subject of my dissertation.

Community psychology as a field was "jelling." The Austin training conference took place during the first part of my graduate school years, but I knew little of the meeting or its recommendations until much later. With the *American Journal of Community Psychology* (AJCP) in its infancy and Division 27 relatively new, there were few formal structures identified with the field. We looked across multiple outlets and disciplines for ideas to advance our thinking and our methods. I remember perusing the university bookstores looking at books assigned for classes in political science, organizational behavior, communication, and education policy among others.

In my therapy practica I struggled with the lack of attention to extra-individual variables and found that this kind of talking treatment had limited applicability to the major mental illnesses such as schizophrenia that I found more interesting. Further, psychotherapy seemed to have little to contribute to my interests in prevention of illness and promotion of mental health. Fortunately for me, the graduate program curriculum required a fixed number of practica but allowed considerable latitude in which practice were completed. After the initial year long practicum in individual talking interventions (aka psychotherapy), I took practice in crisis intervention, program development and evaluation, school consultation, and school-based interventions. I chose to fill the department's requirement for a minor area outside of psychology, taking courses in educational policy, curriculum development, and evaluation. Through these education courses I was exposed to a broad range of participatory, narrative and descriptive methods that were quite distinct from the usual approaches of the psychology department.

My program did not require a formal internship as part of the degree, and I chose not to do one since there weren't internships that would not have required the bulk of time devoted to individual psychotherapy. I knew that this decision could limit future employment options, but I felt that the values and actions of community psychology could be pursued in many different settings. Besides that, I couldn't bear the thought of doing therapy 20 or so hours a week for a year. (Quite a reversal from my career plan senior year in college.) That was just the first time that I told myself I could be happy doing any of a variety of things, and if an internship or a license in psychology were required, well, I just might not be able to be a psychologist. I was willing to take that chance. While there were few models of how and where to pursue this community psychology work that seemed so important, there were also many alternative models such as elected office, public policy centers, community action settings, or even back to my early thoughts of the convent or missionary work.

INTELLECTUAL IDENTITY FORMATION

In 1974 I attended my first APA convention and heard Robert Reiff speak. His talk was stirring and reinforced my blossoming interests in a community action agenda. Several other papers and authors had a lasting effect on my thinking and ultimate career choices. Roger Barker's ecological psychology (1968) and Jim Kelly's writing on social ecology (Kelly, 1970, 1979; Trickett, Kelly, & Todd, 1972) provided a set of constructs for thinking about ecological processes and models for linking settings and individual behavior. Seymour Sarason's *Creation of Settings* (1972) and *The Culture of the School and the Problem of Change* (1974) affected the way I thought about settings, moving beyond earlier mechanistic ideas.

Perhaps the readings that had the greatest impact on my thinking were those of Gregory Bateson and Paul Watzlawick. As an undergraduate I had minored in anthropology. My senior seminar focused on culture and processes of change. We read Bateson among others, but I finished that semester wondering "what the heck was that course was all about." The ideas later came together in a graduate course on systems of psychotherapy and behavior change when I read about therapeutic strategies rooted in paradoxical intentions, and then read Watzlawick, Weakland and Fisch's (1974) book *Change*. These models of system maintenance and change were the theoretical framework for my dissertation on the effects of school desegregation, and continue to influence my thinking.

Ira Levin's science fiction book, *This Perfect Day* (1970), changed my concepts of equality and equity. In this story everyone is equal by virtue of social planning and biological engineering. The story showed equality as sameness and illustrated a state of affairs that was quite distasteful both as I read the book and as I thought about the implications of equality for contemporary issues like school desegregation, affirmative action/equal opportunity, and education for children with disabilities. This novel challenged simplistic notions of equality that I hadn't really thought through and stimulated new thinking about the meaning and shape of equality in our society.

Nevitt Sanford's (1972) chapter "Is the Concept of Prevention Necessary or Useful?" rearranged my thinking about prevention, moving me towards notions of promotion of competence, wellness, and what today we might call positive psychology. Sanford argues that the concept of prevention is stuck in notions of deficiency and illness and because of that will not have a significant impact on mental health at the population level.

With this fairly non-typical perspective, I went on the job market for the first time in 1976 applying for a wide variety of positions including university faculty jobs, program evaluation positions, school psychologist jobs, and a position with the Urban League. The only reciprocated interest or "nibbles" came from universities. I had never been interested in a faculty position during graduate school. I remember arriving at the psychology building early on Saturday mornings and finding quite a few faculty members already there working. I told myself I wasn't going to live my life like that. We attended departmental colloquia and watched faculty rip into each other's work, and I told myself I wasn't going to set myself up for a life with that kind of interaction. I heard the departmental talk about publication rates and how this became equated with personal worth, and I heard the gossip about the "dead wood" in the department, and I told myself I wasn't going to engage in that. So I was disappointed that the only interview invitations I got in 1976 came from university settings, but my mentors told me this was good, the university was a good place to start one's career–plus, I could always leave.

Ironically, I've now spent my entire professional life in a university faculty position (my mother may have had some unique insight when she suggested this as a career option about four decades ago). Perhaps I've rationalized all of this, but I've come to see this as a productive person-environment fit. Throughout my career I've been able to introduce hundreds of students and community-based professionals to contextual models for understanding and enhancing behavior. For the last 20 years I've been affiliated with a clinical-community psychology degree program and had the chance to influence the conceptualization and action models of dozens of mental health professionals, many of whom have gone on to do significant community action work.

The academic setting allowed me to integrate family and career. Acknowledging the horrendous clash of biological and tenure timetables for women in academia, the flexibility and autonomy in day-to-day schedules has allowed me some important advantages. I've been a volunteer in my sons' classrooms, chaperoned many class trips with my children, nearly never missed a concert, awards assembly, game or team banquet. Each of my boys has traveled with me to conferences providing a chance for them to get some idea of what I do through my work, to meet my professional friends, and for us to spend some fun time seeing the sites in the host city. (Interestingly, my oldest son is about to start a doctoral program in American politics with thoughts of becoming a university professor.)

The personal advantages for women in academic settings in terms of balancing work and family are not insignificant. While I have become enmeshed in some of the facets of academia I wanted to avoid (e.g., persistent encroachment on my time and endless work commitments), I've learned about the diversity of academic department environments. I've settled in to friendlier settings. For the last five years I've been chair of a psychology department and have attempted to cultivate a department environment consistent with notions of a healthy community. This experience has been intellectually and emotionally challenging, but more often than not, humbling.

THE CURRENT CONTEXT FOR WOMEN IN COMMUNITY PSYCHOLOGY

Sometimes I wonder if many of the social conditions that propelled action in our field for my generation are no longer so potent. Clearly there are social problems of great magnitude, but it seems there is greater concern with professional identity and status today and that this moderates the weights in our decision-making and may inhibit risk taking for community psychologists. Students today seem more concerned with maintaining access to settings, and less attentive to the benefits of creating alternatives or shaking up a system that they acknowledge is counterproductive. I'm always a little disappointed with graduate students' concerns about acquiring credentials at what seems to be only for the sake of having those credentials. In my own department I see students who say they are pursuing a community psychology track worrying about acquiring specialized therapy training and certificates. When I ask why they are devoting time and money to this, the reply is often something like "you never know when this may be necessary." I'm always thinking, necessary for what that is relevant to *community* psychology?

Students today seem more concerned with titles than we were and more concerned with the degree to which the tasks they are asked to do are commensurate with their advanced training. This attention to status and role is qualitatively different from 25 years ago, and I think may again inhibit risk taking, generation of ideas from direct experience, and full engagement with the community groups and settings that we know to be so important. Dedication and commitment to community work, concern for the collective community good over personal needs toward the prospects of a better world were characteristics I emulated in the nuns who taught me early in life and among my mentors and most valued colleagues. Personal status, titles and credentials were irrelevant, and almost anathema to the most fundamental values of community psychology. Over the last two decades our societal zeitgeist has become more individualistic than collective and certainly our discipline is not immune to the presses of the broader context.

Gender remains one of the most significant organizing schemas in our culture with gender equity still an elusive goal. For me, both the advantages and limitations of my gendered perspective were highlighted by the contrasts with men in my classes and work settings. The massive feminization of psychology, including community psychology, is limiting these opportunities. In terms of career choices, young women today are more aware of the potential conflicts between family and career and seem to be choosing what I would see as more conservative options. I feel old when I hear young women talking about looking for internship or paid positions where their anticipated partner is located. Is the partner cemented to that location forever? Has there been discussion about other options? Can a relationship be a partnership without two-way movement? The social climate of my college experience would have labeled this following behavior in a very negative way. Yet, today there seems to be considerable social support and reinforcement for it. (It makes me want to assign Susan Faludi's (1991) book, *Backlash* as required reading.) I find I'm challenged with how to engage young women in some of these conversations and ways of thinking. Not unlike my own graduate experience, students tell me "I don't want to live my life like you do." I worry that students focus on the negative aspects of academic life and don't have sufficient knowledge or perspective on the totality of the position. Partly in response, I've participated in a monthly women's breakfast involving a few women faculty and graduate students in open-ended conversation about maneuvering through graduate school and dealing with career and life decisions.

I worry about where the next generation of community psychology faculty will come from. Our graduate programs are largely women. For decades we've seen that men are more likely than women to pursue academic employment. If our field is predominantly women and this job-seeking pattern continues to hold, it seems just a matter of time before community psychology will disappear from the halls of academia for lack of faculty. In the 1980's I wrote about this in *The Community Psychologist* (Linney, 1985). While there is certainly much to our field that is done outside of the university, exposure of college students to the concepts and knowledge base seems at least one important ingredient for the continued health of the field. I think we need to focus attention at the very least, on bringing more women into the faculty ranks to continue the work of exposing younger people to this field of inquiry and action. Alternatively, we may need to identify other pathways and mechanisms by which the community perspective will continue to thrive.

As I reflect on my own development as a community psychologist I think there are several salient personal belief systems that have been important in sustaining me, but the presence of validating settings and organizational structures were critically important. The generalized, near automatic tendency to see contextual explanations for behavior has been with me for as long as I can remember. I don't know quite where this came from, but it has clearly been important in keeping me centered as a community psychologist. My work over the years has examined extra-person contextual variables in a number of different developmental groups and problem areas including preschool, elementary and high school settings (Linney, 1984; 1989), programs for juvenile offenders (Linney, 1982), people with serious mental illness (Linney, Arns, Chinman & Frank, 1995), and multiracial neighborhoods (Berryhill & Linney, 2000). I've tended to take advantage of opportunities presenting themselves and have not had a singular interest in a particular problem or group. My "near aversion" to working at the individual level to solve broader problems renews itself regularly. Life experiences have given me a fundamental confidence in my capacity to survive just about whatever comes along. I think that allows me to pursue the unknown and to sustain effort. At the same time, I find that I have considerable respect for the complexity of social problems and recognize that solutions are not likely to be forthcoming, will require a long term perspective, and that the process is as important as any outcome. I do like to see the effects of my effort, but like the nuns I admired in elementary school, I'm not completely dependent on that to keep me going. I was a competitive figure skater for 10 years and learned from the vagaries of the judging process that effort, skill, performance and outcome are not necessarily in a predictable relationship. Rather there are many intangibles and factors outside one's control that can determine the results. These were good lessons for a career in community psychology, and in fact can stimulate enhanced understanding of systemic processes. My father often consoled us after a bitter competitive defeat with the belief that things have a way of working out for the best, there will be another day, and there is only limited value in dwelling on the disappointment. These have proven to be valuable beliefs for a community psychologist.

The values and perspectives underlying my community psychology identity were probably seeded prior to formal study, but exposure to written work, engagement with supportive mentors, flexible program structures, and the availability of the university setting enabled development of these ideas, provided a name and a set of methods for the activities, and a formal validating structure. Whatever my contribution to the field, it has been exciting and fun. I think my husband and my boys are happy the convent wasn't the path I took instead.

REFERENCES

Barker, R. (1968). *Ecological psychology*. Stanford, CA: Stanford University Press.
Berryhill, J. & Linney, J. A. (2000). Empowering citizens in an impoverished multiethnic community. *Journal of the Community Development Society*, 31, 233-253.
Faludi, S. (1991). *Backlash: The undeclared war against American women*. New York: Doubleday.
Kelly, J. G. (1970). Toward an ecological conception of preventive interventions. In D. Adelson & B. Kalis (Eds.), *Community psychology and mental health* (pp. 126-145). Scranton, PA: Chandler.
Kelly, J. G. (Ed.) (1979). *Adolescent boys in high school: A psychological study of coping and adaptation*. Hillsdale, NJ: Erlbaum.
Levin, I. (1970). *This perfect day*. New York: Dell.
Linney, J. A. (1982). "Alternative" facilities for youth in trouble: Descriptive analysis of a strategically selected sample. In J. Handler & J. Zatz (Eds.), *Neither Angels nor Thieves: Studies in Deinstitutionalization of Status Offenders* (pp. 127-175). Washington, D. C.: National Academy Press.
Linney, J. A. (1984). Deinstitutionalization in the juvenile justice system. In N. D. Reppucci, L. A. Weithorn, E. P. Mulvey, & J. Monahan (Eds.), *Mental Health, Law and Children* (pp. 211-231). Beverly Hills, CA: Sage.

Linney, J. A. (1985, Fall). Community psychology and women: Visibility for an invisible "subject." *The Community Psychologist.*

Linney, J. A. (1986). Court ordered school desegregation: Shuffling the deck or playing a different game. In E. Seidman and J. Rappaport (Eds.), *Redefining Social Problems* (pp. 259-274). New York: Plenum.

Linney, J. A., Arns, P. G., Chinman, M., & Frank, J. (1995). Priorities in community residential care: A comparison of operators and mental health consumers. *Psychosocial Rehabilitation Journal, 19*, 27-34.

Linney, J. A. & Seidman, E. (1989). The future of schooling. *American Psychologist, 44*, 336-340.

Sanford, N. (1972). Is the concept of prevention necessary or useful? In S. Golann and C. Eisdorfer (Eds.), *Handbook of community mental health.* New York: Appleton-Century-Crofts.

Sarason, S. B. (1972). *The creation of settings and the future societies.* San Francisco: Jossey-Bass.

Sarason, S. B. (1974). *The culture of the school and the problem of change.* Boston: Allyn & Bacon.

Trickett, E. J., Kelly, J.G., & Todd, D. M. (1972). The social environment of the school: Guidelines for individual change and organizational redevelopment. In S. Golann and C. Eisdorfer (Eds.), *Handbook of community mental health* (pp. 331-406). New York: Appleton-Century-Crofts.

Watzlawick, P., Weakland, J., & Fisch, R. (1974). *Change: Principles of problem formation and problem resolution.* New York: Norton.

Ecological Influences on an Ecologically-Oriented Community Psychologist

Marybeth Shinn

New York University

SUMMARY. My development as an ecologically-oriented community psychologist was shaped by many ecologies, including my family's religious faith, the civil rights, anti-war, and feminist movements, and the diverse cultures I have been privileged to experience. Harvard's Social Relations department and Michigan's programs in Social and Community Psychology provided intellectual underpinnings for an ecological viewpoint. New York University's program in Community Psychology and New York itself have allowed a variety of exciting research opportunities. Sexism has also shaped my career, and combining work and family has been sometimes a challenge, but always a joy. *[Article copies available for a fee from The Haworth Document Delivery Service: 1-800-HAWORTH. E-mail address: <docdelivery@haworthpress.com> Website: <http://www.HaworthPress.com> © 2004 by The Haworth Press, Inc. All rights reserved.]*

Address correspondence to: Beth Shinn, Department of Psychology, 6 Washington Place, Room 275, New York, NY 10003 (E-mail: beth.shinn@nyu.edu).

The author thanks Jim Kelly for initiating this project, and for thoughtful comments on earlier versions of this manuscript.

[Haworth co-indexing entry note]: "Ecological Influences on an Ecologically-Oriented Community Psychologist." Shinn, Marybeth. Co-published simultaneously in *Journal of Prevention & Intervention in the Community* (The Haworth Press, Inc.) Vol. 28, No. 1/2, 2004, pp. 103-124; and: *Six Community Psychologists Tell Their Stories: History, Contexts, and Narrative* (eds: James G. Kelly, and Anna V. Song) The Haworth Press, Inc., 2004, pp. 103-124. Single or multiple copies of this article are available for a fee from The Haworth Document Delivery Service [1-800-HAWORTH, 9:00 a.m. - 5:00 p.m. (EST). E-mail address: docdelivery@haworthpress.com].

http://www.haworthpress.com/web/JPIC
© 2004 by The Haworth Press, Inc. All rights reserved.
Digital Object Identifier: 10.1300/J005v28n01_06

KEYWORDS. Community Psychology, Ecology, feminism, diversity, civil rights, anti-war

The last time I wrote an autobiographical essay was in elementary school. I can still remember my teacher's dismay at my opening line, about how I had been a troublemaker even before I was born. (My untimely arrival forced the obstetrician to miss his lunch). "Who told you that?" she demanded, appalled at the deep psychological damage this interpretation implied. She didn't realize that troublemaker was a valued social identity for a future community psychologist. Beginning with elementary school, I have tried to change almost every setting I have joined.

FAMILY

Education

I was born in November, 1951 into a family that valued education. My father was teaching at Heidelberg College, a small denominationally-affiliated school in Ohio, which both my parents and my grandparents had attended, while he completed his dissertation. In those days before computers and photocopy machines, he kept the dissertation manuscript, swathed in protective coverings, in the refrigerator, as the safest place in our firetrap of a house. He joked that in case of fire, he did not want to feel conflicted between grabbing a child and grabbing his dissertation. As he moved up the academic ladder at Vanderbilt Divinity School and Union Theological Seminary, an interdenominational Protestant seminary affiliated with Columbia University, we moved to Nashville and then to New York. I grew up in the Seminary's faculty housing from the age of seven.

Our house was overflowing with books, and my older sister and I were voracious readers. Thirty years later, when we lived in the same neighborhood, my children could still find book cards with my name entered in the borrower column at the Morningside Junior Library, in obscure books that had not drawn much attention over the years. My father was a prolific scholar, who, when at home, could most often be found in his study working on a book or an article. Although we did not have a lot of money, and my parents, who grew up in the Depression, were frugal with what we had, nothing was spared with respect to education. It was clear that I was expected to do well at school.

Religion

My father was an ordained minister, as was his father before him, and he taught Christian ethics. Religious faith was central to my family, with a liberal emphasis on social justice, combined with a strict personal morality. One of my grandmothers was a stalwart of the Women's Christian Temperance Union. I wrote my confirmation essay on differences between Protestantism and Catholicism, because I rather envied the Catholic distinction between venial and mortal sin, and the clear route to absolution. For us it seemed that all infractions were mortal, and forgiveness never certain. The parts of my religious upbringing that have stuck with me are the concern with social justice, the moral imperative to act like the Good Samaritan, to alleviate suffering, and the sense that any talents or privileges I might have were gifts that brought obligations "for unto whomsoever much is given, of him shall be much required." It was not clear whether, as a girl, I would work outside the home, but it was clear that any role, whether volunteer or paid, should be not merely an occupation, or even a profession, but a vocation.

Gender Roles

My nuclear family adhered to traditional gender roles. Although my parents had graduated from the same college with the same honors, my father took the prestigious professional job; my mother was a homemaker and professor's wife. The latter role could be quite demanding–the year my father served as acting president of the seminary, my mother served nearly 1,100 guests in our home. She was also active in volunteer work, although this never received the attention at the dinner table that my father's work did. As I grew older she held a succession of part-time "faculty wife" jobs. Before the women's movement opened up additional roles to talented women, universities used to run on the inexpensive labor of faculty wives–intelligent women who understood academic norms and local history and who could actually get faculty members to fulfill their obligations, in part because they interacted with them in other social contexts. Women were far less likely to serve as members of the faculty.

My father's younger sister provided an alternative feminist role model, although I didn't label it so at the time. She had gone to college during World War II, when most men were off at the front, and then had spent three years teaching at a girls' school in Turkey (a bold move for a young woman at the time). Thus she completely missed the post-war advertising campaign to get women out of the factories and back to their rightful place behind brand-name vacuum cleaners, electric mixers, and smiling children. She never married, but held a series of interesting jobs for the YWCA (promoting leadership for college women) and later the Women's Bureau of the Department of Labor. Her life seemed full of exciting stories, such as swimming across the Bosporus between the continents of Europe and Asia. She had shown more than a hint of rebelliousness against both parents and social mores. (I remember accompanying her to distribute campaign literature from a local reform democratic party in apartment buildings until we got thrown out by a doorman, and marveling at her equanimity in the face of being caught in this horrendous violation of rules). It seemed to me as a teenager that my choices were to get married and be a homemaker like my mother or to forgo marriage and children and have an activist career like my aunt. The career was far more attractive.

I might have seen another option in my mother's younger sister's career. She earned a PhD in biology, married one of her instructors, and collaborated with him in both parenting and a scientific career as an ornithologist. However, he was the professor, and she was barred by university nepotism rules from the kinds of positions she might otherwise have held. I was not much interested in birds, but did want to follow her in being a scientist or mathematician. (In the post-Sputnik era, science counted as a vocation). I was given a chemistry set, and somehow acquired the remnants of another second hand. I convinced myself I was doing "real" experiments, not simply following cookbook directions, by mixing chemicals from the two different sets.

HIGH SCHOOL, COLLEGE, AND THE LARGER SOCIAL CONTEXT

The Depression and World War II had shaped my parents' generation. I came of age in turbulent political times and was deeply influenced by three political movements and their antecedents. In order of my awareness, these were: racism and the Civil Rights movement, the Vietnam War and the peace movement, and sexism and the feminist movement. I also experienced a number of different cultures as I grew up, first by chance and later by choice.

Racism and Civil Rights

When I started first grade in Nashville, Tennessee in 1956, two years after *Brown v. Board of Education*, Ransom School was still all White.

There was a plan to have one Black child come into the first grade my year, so the two classes were formed by dividing families who might be actively hostile from families who "wouldn't mind." Mine was the more liberal group. My parents tried to prepare me for the big event by explaining that others might react negatively, but that such racism was wrong. It never came off. I do not know whether racists prevailed, or whether more responsible adults decided that the burden of desegregating a school with over 300 White students, some of them hostile, should not rest entirely on the shoulders of a single Black five or six-year old.

We moved to New York in 1958, between second and third grade, when my father joined Union Seminary, located on the border of Harlem. Now my school, P.S. 125, was almost entirely Black. Racism played out differently in the North. The half dozen or so White children per year were all placed in the class for "Intellectually Gifted Children" (IGC). One of the privileges accorded us periodically was to skip classes to run errands for the school office. There I observed prospective students being interviewed about dolls–a policeman (no women here), a fireman, and a milkman dressed in white and carrying a wooden case with six milk bottles. Even at the time, I thought of this as the "Golden Book" test, since milkmen did not emerge from the pages of such books to walk the streets of Harlem. Although it seems hard to credit as an adult, my understanding at the time was that placement in the tracked classes depended on children's ability to identify and talk about these dolls. Even then this seemed profoundly unjust.

The school was badly overcrowded. By the time I graduated there were 9 sixth grades and perhaps 14 first grades, with the younger students on a split schedule, so that they got only half a day of schooling. There was no gym equipment and we rarely had physical education. We had regular fallout drills, which mostly meant walking quietly down to the basement, in double lines of girls and boys organized by size, for protection against nuclear bombs. On one occasion when a teacher miscounted the number of bells in the signal we were instead directed to hide from the bombs beneath our classroom desks. Perhaps the absurdity of the situation meant that I never took it all that seriously.

Despite the lack of resources, at least the IGC class offered a strong education. My sixth grade teacher required boys to wear ties and all children to carry handkerchiefs, enforced discipline by hitting desks and sometimes children with her ruler, and had us recite poems in unison with such stylized intonation that my older sister, who had her three years earlier, and I could recite together. She was nevertheless a gifted and creative teacher. We spent the first 20 minutes of every day on a writing assignment. We voted on the genres and changed them from time to time–Monday was a newspaper column, Tuesday a limerick, Wednesday a short story and so forth. Fellow students gave feedback. Reading was with an experimental self-paced curriculum, and we were all well beyond grade level. When I later went to private school, I had to wait a year for my class to catch up in math. Sixth graders "adopted" first grade classes and regularly read to them (with half of us as readers and half as illustrators of the selected texts). For assemblies we wrote and performed skits about favorite books.

I even had my first touch of successful activism. The school decided that since there were insufficient seats in the auditorium for all sixth graders to invite two relatives for graduation, each child would be permitted just one guest. I ran home at lunchtime and typed up a petition asking that children who wanted two tickets be given them, since not all children could use two. By the end of the post-lunch recess, I had gathered dozens of signatures. The school readily agreed, and my father, who no doubt would have preferred to leave the event to my mother, had to attend.

My older sister had gotten into some trouble in the local junior high school, and my parents decided I should attend a private school for junior high and high school. The population at Riverdale was very different from either the all-White Nashville or nearly all-Black New York schools I had attended. For the first time I had Jewish friends (I had reached seventh grade in New York City without ever tasting a bagel), and classmates with considerable wealth. Wealth is the one dimension of diversity with which I have never gotten comfortable. Between my family's social conservatism and relatively modest means, I could not keep up with classmates in dress or activities. I compensated by taking all sorts of part-time jobs as baby sitter, building attendant, switchboard operator, sales clerk, and substitute receptionist in a doctor's office to earn money.

During this period I was horrified by the violence against civil rights demonstrators in the South and thrilled by stories of resistance by Rosa Parks and Martin Luther King, Jr. My personal involvement extended only to boycotting the local Woolworth's because the chain had refused to serve African Americans in the South and boycotting grapes (a bigger sacrifice) to support the farm workers. My understanding of the Civil Rights movement was definitely circumscribed by white liberalism. I read Martin Luther King, Jr.'s speeches, but knew nothing of Malcolm X; similarly I knew more about the White Freedom Riders from the north than about the Black organizers of Freedom Summer in Mississippi.

War and the Peace Movement

As I progressed through high school, the United States got more deeply involved in Vietnam, and protests erupted on campuses. We lived near Columbia, where students occupied buildings during my senior year (1968-69). I got involved in some anti-war protests in high school. Meanwhile my father began talking for the first time about his experiences during World War II. He had given up his exemption from the draft as a seminary student, got commissioned as a "90-day wonder," and was a company commander when he was captured trying to reach soldiers who had been cut off in the Battle of the Bulge. My mother, who was pregnant, lost their first child when he was reported missing and presumed dead. In the late 60's my father worked with the ACLU defending soldiers who refused to fight in Vietnam although they did not qualify as conscientious objectors, because they were not pacifists or did not subscribe to organized religions. He was an effective witness in court martial proceedings–he had won a Silver Star for actions before he was captured and mustered out of the army as a Major, so could not be dismissed by the military officers who sat in judgment. Nevertheless, the defendants lost every case. He wrote a book based on his wartime diaries and later theological reflections on war and the men he defended. I had a teenager's unreasonable scorn for my father's role in the Civil Rights movement–he eventually got himself arrested in a protest when (it seemed to me) that no self-respecting liberal theologian could fail to have an arrest record. But I was proud of his work defending men who refused to fight in Vietnam. This work provided a model for my own activism, seeking places where one's particular array of talents or experiences provide the most leverage.

I got much more active in the anti-war movement in college, participating in strikes on campus and helping (in a minor way) to organize protests in Boston and Washington. Young men faced terrible choices. One in my dorm starved himself to stay below the weight limit for the draft, until he contracted tuberculosis. Others took advantage of wealth and privilege to pay doctors to diagnose esoteric conditions that kept them out, or played on homophobia in draft boards. Several considered moving to Canada, before being rescued by lucky draws in the draft lottery. I wondered whether I would have the courage to do what I thought I should do, had I been male, namely to refuse the draft and go to jail. Our government seemed morally bankrupt, forsaking the idealism projected by Kennedy and the War on Poverty furthered by Johnson for a war on impoverished peasants halfway around the globe.

Sexism and Feminism

I experienced the effects of sexism in much more direct ways than racism or militarism, but did not always label it as such. I was a tomboy growing up, the girl who would get invited to boys' birthday parties when their mothers insisted that they have at least one girl. Everyone from the first grade teacher, who told me that little girls don't play at the top of the jungle gym, to my grandmother, who told me that I really ought to let my high school boyfriend beat me in ping pong, attempted (unsuccessfully) to correct my lack of proper feminine demeanor.

I also violated the rule that girls should not be good at math. Going to a girls' high school initially provided a protective environment for excelling in math. In 11th grade, the school decided to hold joint boys' school and girls' school classes in math to allow more levels of instruction–there were just 4 girls in the honors class. Between 11th and 12th grades I attended a National Science Foundation summer program in mathematics, where only the handful of girls were subjected to a curfew. In 12th grade I was the only girl in the more advanced calculus class and in physics. Worse, since at the boys' school physics was taken in 11th grade, they put me as a senior in with junior boys. What humiliation!

College was worse. I entered Radcliffe/Harvard in the fall of 1969 with sophomore standing so declared math as a major from the outset. I was immediately faced with a choice between the regular class in second year calculus and linear algebra or the more challenging Math 55. The guys (they were all guys) in the mathematics department's peer advisement told me that no woman had ever successfully taken Math 55 (a fact I learned later to be false). I thought the admissions committee had made a mistake in taking me to begin with (no girl from my high school had been admitted for the past three years), and did not have the courage to try the more difficult course. Then my assigned faculty advisor in math (who did not know my name, so could not have been offering advice on the basis of any rational assessment of my talents) suggested that I leave mathematics because, in his opinion, the only reason a woman should major in math was in order to marry a mathematician. Feminism was in the air, but it had not yet wafted down to me. My (silent) reaction was not "I'll show you, you male chauvinist pig," but "who would want to marry you?" I was totally demoralized and seriously considered dropping out of college as I cast about for a different major, and planned a leave of absence for the following fall.

Luckily, for my intellectual development, Harvard at the time had an undergraduate major in Social Relations, which combined social anthropology, sociology, and the social end of psychology. I took a first anthropology course (on primitive religions) pass-fail on a lark in the fall of my first year, and was entranced; by spring, when I also had psychology, I had decided that Social Relations would be my new major. The training in anthropology and sociology was a wonderful background for an ecologically-oriented psychologist. I read Goffman's (1961) *Asylums* and did volunteer work my first year in a back ward of a state mental hospital, where long-term patients were classic examples of institutionalization.

The following summer, 1970, I took part in a Western Interstate Commission on Higher Education summer program on the sociology of mental health with a placement in the day-treatment unit of a community mental health center in San Jose. This was an important formative experience. It was fascinating and fun (I could hardly believe that I was getting paid), but it seemed to me that our mode of treatment, which involved removing people from the problematic situations in their lives and putting them into the protected environment of the center, was bound to fail. We had only a piece of the problem (the individual in pain), and could not hope to change the problem itself without the other actors. At best, we patched people up and sent them back into the fray. At worst, the style of interaction we taught in group therapy (open expression of negative feelings, confrontation of people who denied their problems) seemed likely to cause trouble with bosses, spouses, and others who had not been socialized to the center's norms. I had not started to think of prevention, but began as an undergraduate to develop an ecological critique of clinical psychology.

I returned from my leave in the spring of 1971 energized, and ready to make use of what Harvard had to offer, from passionate intellectual and political discussions with other students around the dinner table to a faculty who took undergraduates seriously. I served on the Committee on Undergraduate Education and worked (with political scientist James Q. Wilson) to institute the first course evaluations at Harvard. Physicist (and later Nobel Laureate) Norman Ramsey took each of the student members of the committee to lunch individually to hear our views.

I recall one experience that shows how much campus life has changed for women. My senior year (1972-73) I was in New Haven, when I ran into the Radcliffe women's basketball team, down to play Yale. They were short-handed, and asked me to join them. I had not been good enough play for my high school, but they were desperate. They had spare uniforms, so my participation hinged on whether they could come up with the right sized sneakers. They couldn't, so although I claim, on the strength of this experience, to have been *recruited* by a Division I basketball team, I never played.

I had taken personality psychology from Matina Horner, whose ideas about fear of success resonated with me (e.g., Horner, 1970). The idea was that in "male" fields where women are not expected to succeed, they anticipate adverse consequences for success, internalize these, and hence curtail their performance. She agreed to sponsor my undergraduate thesis, which I began in the spring of 1972, although when she was appointed President of Radcliffe shortly afterward, there were more competing demands for her time than either of us had anticipated. The high school I had attended was going co-educational, and they allowed me to come back to observe the process. I tested both boys and girls in separate classes before the transition and in co-educational classes a year later, and found that girls' fear of success, coded from a projective measure, rose and their performance on paper and pencil tasks declined. Further, the rise in fear of success was correlated with the decline in performance. (Boys did not show a parallel rise in fear of failure, operationalized as test anxiety). These findings were alarming to me and to the school (although they may have been due to the change, rather than to the state of coeducation, and were certainly influenced by a set of sex-role attitudes that one hopes have disappeared). Naturally the school wanted to know what to do. I talked to a number of August faculty members in Social Relations, who had no idea. To me it seemed morally irresponsible to walk away from the school after uncovering a problem; to them research was an end in itself, with no particular implications for action, and in any case, they had no relevant expertise.

Psychologists a generation older than I invented the field of community psychology. Like many in my generation, I re-invented some of the elements for myself before discovering that there was such a field. By the end of college I had a strong ecological orientation, shaped by undergraduate coursework in anthropology and sociology as well as psychology, and by experiences in the mental health system and in research. I also had a clear orientation towards action, motivated by my research, and a strong sense of social justice, shaped by my upbringing and the social movements of the time. I knew I wanted to study community psychology, I simply did not know what it was called or where to find it. But first I was off to Africa. I took a second leave of absence (permitted by my initial entry with sophomore standing) in the spring of 1973 while finishing my undergraduate thesis, and learned Swahili.

Diversity

I have already mentioned vastly different demographic profiles of my first three schools. My high school had a program that permitted students to study abroad for a third of the tenth grade year, and I went to France. The students met up at the end of the school year and traveled in Europe, under the supervision of a teacher. So when I took my first leave of absence from college in 1970, I wanted to return to Europe to travel on my own. My parents permitted me to go on the condition that I spend the first two months studying at a language school (a Goethe Institute) in Germany. There were more Libyans than any other nationality in my class, and I hung out mostly with Turks, who formed the majority at the Institute.

In 1973-74, between college and graduate school, I had a fellowship to study the changing role of women in Kenya, and spent a year teaching school in a rural area, many miles from pavement, electricity, or running water. (Where water has to be carried on women's heads, one soon learns that it is always found at the *bottom* of the hill). I was the first Mzungu (White person) many people in the area had seen, and on several occasions, little children burst into tears at the sight of me. Mary Douglas's (1966) brilliant little book on the dangers of liminality (things on the borders of known categories) helped me understand that in their eyes my pale, ghostlike appearance made me almost human but not quite. I became aware, as I had not, growing up in New York, of how powerful a stimulus race is, even to people who have not been trained, as we are in our society, in racism. And for the first time in my life I was continually aware of my race (as must be the case for visible minorities in the U.S.), as people touched my hair, were fascinated by the pale stripe under my watchband (did I wear the watch there to hide it?), and pushed up my sleeve (to see whether my skin eventually got normal or stayed that funny color everywhere). After several months, when I visited Nairobi, the White folks there looked odd to me as well.

The situation of a local man who was probably schizophrenic led me to a deeper understanding of contextual issues in mental illness. (The local diagnosis was that his mother had cursed him at his birth). On the one hand, his social inappropriateness, dazed appearance, and inability to care for himself made me realize that the symptoms I had seen in the back wards could not all be attributed to institutionalization. On the other hand, he led a life with few restrictions, cared for by the community as a whole–he could wander into any conversation, and be fed at any hearth. His freedom gave new meaning to the idea of care in "the least restrictive environment," and probably influenced my later interest in deinstitutionalization, and in housing people who have been homeless in apartments with few restrictions.

I was conflicted over political activism in Kenya. My feminist values led me to want to challenge female circumcision, polygamy, and favoritism towards males in schooling. (The first two were indigenous, but the latter was due to Europeans who initially established formal schools only for boys). But it was clear that Kenya, only recently liberated from colonialism, had to be led by Kenyans. I had taken the epigraph of my undergraduate thesis from Umoja wa Wanawake wa Tanzania (Tanzania's major national women's organization). The organization had drawn an analogy between the legacies of belief in one's own inferiority that colonialism and sexism both leave in their victims–the link to fear of success was evident. In the immediate post-colonial period, political activism by a Mzungu or even a group that included a Mzungu would be counterproductive in direct proportion to its success, if it strengthened the misperception that foreign leadership was necessary for progress. I had not yet heard of empowerment, but had encountered the dilemma of empowering others who had been disenfranchised.

My return to the United States in the fall of 1974 was more jarring than my initial trip to Kenya. I had expected Africa to be different; but after two previous trips abroad I had not expected to see my own country, particularly our consumer culture, through such different lenses on my return. After living in a country with no waste baskets (because there is nothing to throw away) and where clean water was a luxury, I was confronted with super stores and shopping malls. Americans seemed abysmally ignorant of the rest of the world and oblivious to the way that we were seen beyond our own borders. It was hard to integrate the different worlds.

GRADUATE SCHOOL

I entered the social psychology program at the University of Michigan in 1974. The Psychology and Sociology departments at Michigan had traditionally run a joint program in social psychology, although this had recently been disbanded, and the Research Center for Group Dynamics had been the home of Kurt Lewin and action research. Thus I hoped to learn tools to understand and change social settings. (There was a fortuitous aspect to the choice as well. I had written to several schools shortly before I left for Kenya, stating my credentials, and asking them to allow me to apply before I lost access to a typewriter. Most places said applications were not accepted at that time of year but a secretary at Michigan read my letter, sent me the forms, and promised to shepherd my application through. I never met her, but she convinced me that my fear that Michigan would be large and anonymous was unfounded).

I was able to pursue my goal of learning to change settings. In my first year I worked on an experimental intervention with Bob Caplan and Jack French to help patients adhere to anti-hypertensive regimens by increasing patient education and social support (i.e., by changing the context within which medical care was provided). Caplan focused me on social support, and French taught me the concept of person-environment fit. Henry Ford hospital in Detroit, where we did the work, reminded me of sex role expectations, with staff bathrooms labeled Doctors and Nurses.

I also learned something about the weakness of quantitative analyses that fail to take contextual information into account. Our analyses suggested that interventions based on patient education and social support did indeed lead to increased perceptions of support and adherence to medical regimens, but, contrary to prediction, the social support condition was no better than mere education. Then a nurse, Retha Flowers, joined the doctoral program and the project, and explained that, although blood pressure in millimeters of mercury might appear to be an interval-level measure, from the perspective of doctors, it was either in control or out of control. This nominal distinction led to vastly different treatment for patients. Patients whose blood pressure was in control did not need to be seen often. But those whose blood pressure was out of control experienced frequent visits, changes in medication regimens, and general tension and flux. When the data were reanalyzed considering blood pressure as a nominal variable, the superiority of the social support condition became apparent.

Dorwin (Doc) Cartwright agreed to give me a reading course on Lewin and Barker (neither were part of the regular curriculum). Field Theory, the collection of Lewin's essays that Cartwright had edited was out of print so I photocopied his copy. I felt as though I had been blessed by direct apostolic descent. Bob Zajonc was developing his confluence theory of how the number and spacing of children affects the average intellectual environment of the family and hence predicts children's cognitive growth. He hired me as a research assistant and assigned me to do a literature review on the effects of growing up in a single-parent home on children's cognitive development. However, he was at the Advanced

Center in Palo Alto the year I worked with him, so we had little interaction. James Jackson was just gearing up for the Black Americans view their mental health study by the time I was leaving Ann Arbor. Dan Katz and Bob Kahn brought out the second edition of *the Social Psychology of Organizations*.

Some of my fellow students in social psychology were also interested in social contexts or interventions. Irma Serrano-Garcia went on to do community psychology in Puerto Rico. Sally Shumaker studied environmental psychology in graduate school and went on to do health psychology and play a major role in the women's health initiative. Dick Moreland later studied the transmission of norms across generations in groups. But for the most part, social psychology in the mid 1970s ignored broader social contexts in favor of lab experiments designed to understand cognitive processes. I asked Dan Katz, who had been active in early social psychological work to challenge racial stereotypes and promote cross-race interaction, "why?" He said that social psychologists had been naive in their initial approaches to intervention. They thought they could make the world a better place, and felt burned when the world did not necessarily want to be intervened upon and improved under the direction of social psychologists. As a result, most retreated to the safety of the psychology lab.

Luckily for me, Michigan also had a small community program, staffed by Rick Price (who arrived the same year I did) and Cary Cherniss. I ended up completing this as well as the social program, and doing my dissertation with Cherniss. Seymour Sarason (with whom Cherniss had worked) and Rudy Moos (with whom Price had worked) were probably the two most central theorists we read (e.g., Moos, 1974, Sarason, 1974), but I also remember intellectually exciting visits from Julian Rappaport and Ed Trickett (who talked during the day and then sang at night at the Ark, a local house for folk-music), and readings about neighborhoods (e.g., Warren & Warren, 1977).

My central training experience in graduate school was probably the Youth Home Development Project, which Cary Cherniss, Dennis Perkins, and I started in my first year. I was definitely the junior member of the team. Perkins, a student in the organizational psychology program who also joined the community area, was only a year ahead of me in school, but far ahead in life, having resigned his commission in the Navy over Vietnam, and gotten an MBA at Harvard before coming to Michigan. I learned a great deal from him. The idea of the project was to help group homes and halfway houses for youth to improve their social climates via a survey-guided development process, inspired both by Moos's work (e.g., Moos, 1973) and by the organizational development literature (e.g., Bowers, 1973). A team of two consultants fed back data to participants on discrepancies between real and ideal social and work climates and used this as a basis for problem solving and goal setting. After piloting the change process in three homes, we set up an experimental evaluation, in which homes all over Michigan and northern Ohio were blocked into pairs and randomly assigned to treatment or a delayed treatment control condition. Cherniss, Perkins, and I became "senior" consultants who paired with other graduate students to do the projects in new homes; those who had been through one complete change cycle were then senior consultants, who could train new people. We also partnered with "in-house consultants" at the homes, to whom we tried to give away the process. The overall evaluation became my dissertation, and others did MA theses. I learned an enormous amount about small organizations and their internal dynamics, about how quantitative data (the climate scores) could be augmented by qualitative information (in subsequent meetings), and about social change. The intervention was moderately successful, but hampered by staff turnover, which exceeded 200% per year in some homes. This contributed to Cherniss's interest in staff burnout in human service settings, and led me to study similar phenomena in my first job post PhD.

Women were still in the minority in psychology graduate school (that was beginning to change in clinical and developmental, but not elsewhere), and there were only a few women faculty. I participated in several women's groups, which focused variously on gender roles, mutual support, and political action. We got data from the Psychology Department suggesting that over the past five years, most areas had consistently admitted a lower proportion of women than in their applicant pools. We presented the data to each of the area directors to ask them not to discriminate against women, getting generally positive receptions.

All in all, Michigan was a wonderful place to be a graduate student, because of its intellectual diversity. My faculty in social psychology were tolerant of my involvement in community psychology, as they were tolerant when I took scuba diving lessons or spent a summer at the National Institute of Mental Health, helping to launch the Community Support Program to provide community-based services for people with serious and persistent mental illnesses. I also learned from faculty in organizational behavior and developmental psychology and took courses in social work and public health. But Ann Arbor itself was far less diverse. For example, the best foreign restaurant in town was a hole in the wall called Steve's Lunch, which served Korean specialties along with steak and eggs. I was eager to return to a more cosmopolitan city.

By the end of graduate school, I was not sure whether I wanted an academic or more activist job, but decided to try academia first, on the grounds that switches out of the academy would be easier than switches in. I looked only at community programs, and chose New York University for the opportunity to return to the City as well as for the job itself. New York seemed a more comfortable place for me as a single woman than some of the alternatives.

FIRST JOB

NYU had a small, freestanding community program. The other program faculty, Stan Lehmann and Barbara Felton, were enormously supportive and welcoming; the department chair was not. He assigned me to various tasks no one else wanted, such as teaching in a satellite program in Westchester. At NYU, a dissertation committee consists of just three people, with two readers tacked on at the time of orals. When I drove east in my U-Haul truck in August, 1978, an NYU student, Patricia O'Connor, was trying desperately to get hold of me because I had been assigned as a reader for her dissertation (a week before I flew back to Ann Arbor to defend my own). Over my first two years I served in some capacity on 33 theses and dissertations, due both to the understaffing in the program and to continual assignments by the chair. I did not realize I could say no. (I should note that we have a far better faculty-student ratio and are much kinder to junior faculty today).

Another assignment from the chair–to teach the MA statistics class my first fall–worked out better. I went to a mathematical psychologist, David Krantz, from whom I had had my first-year statistics class at Michigan, for advice. He had later asked me to teach statistics with him, but I had fellowship support and a friend wanted the job, so I had declined. We'd chatted some over the years, and he had helped me with a data analysis problem, but I did not know him terribly well. David was generous in helping me plan the course I would teach, and as I left, I suggested he should look me up if he were ever in New York. He did, and we soon became a couple, marrying in January 1981. As it turned out, I married a mathematician without even majoring in mathematics.

Our relationship led me to get a small dose of the humiliating process that many women who get involved with more senior men still go through–the search for the spousal job. Naturally, we hoped to find jobs that would allow us to live together. David was far better known than I, so there were a number of universities that were interested in him, if they could figure out what to do with me. I had a number of conversations and gave a couple of job talks at universities that had no real interest in community psychology or in me. One department chair wrote me that although my work was very interesting, "it is outside the field of psychology, as we define it." Even at a university with a community program, we never got as far as the talking stage because I got the impression that I would be seen as an appendage to David. Two factors mitigated the adverse effect of this process on my self-esteem. First, I had landed the faculty job at NYU and gotten other offers before David was in the picture. My initial job search had been untinged by sexism. Second, David was able to generate several offers in the New York area, and took a job at Bell Labs, later moving to Columbia, so that I could stay at NYU. Many women are not so lucky in their timing or their partner's ability to move, and as long as more junior women get involved with more senior men, the pain in this process will fall disproportionately on female shoulders.

NYU was not a bad place to be a woman–there were women faculty at all ranks in the department, and one of my two senior colleagues in community psychology was a woman. But some stereotypes die hard. A senior male faculty member handed another junior woman, hired at the same time I was, his photocopying to do, on the assumption that she was a new secretary. The director of our Office of Sponsored Programs (a woman) was convinced that I was turned down for a grant from the National Institute of Mental Health because I was a woman, on the basis of what she felt were deprecating comments in the pink sheets (reviews), but I got the same study funded by the National Science Foundation instead.

I was probably more conscious of my youth than of my gender. I had completed only seven years of schooling post high school (spread over 9 years, with two semester leaves of absence in college and the year in Kenya between college and graduate school), and was 26 when I started in 1978. It took about five years for me to reach the median age of students in the doctoral program, who often came to us with substantial outside experience. At first when anyone called me "Dr. Shinn," I looked around for my father. I had not had a great deal of teaching experience in graduate school, and the first time I walked into my undergraduate community psychology class with 50 students, it was all I could do not to turn around and walk back out.

I was naive in another way that may be linked to both age and gender. In graduate school, it seemed the height of hubris to send off anything for publication, and I did so only under clear directives from faculty. I sent an article version of my undergraduate thesis to the Association of Women in Psychology because the prize (which I won) for best student paper was a trip to the American Psychological Association in San Francisco, but I never sent it to a journal. Even as a faculty member, it never occurred to me until after I had tenure to revise and re-submit either a manuscript or a grant proposal that was not accepted (perhaps with minor revisions) on the initial submission. At that point I had a longer list of unpublished than of published manuscripts, and many of my publications were in special journal issues, where reviewers were kinder. My doctoral dissertation appeared in conference proceedings, but I never revised it after a journal editor said there were altogether too many diagrams full of boxes and arrows in the literature, and I should remove the one in my paper. It was not until I served as associate editor for the *American Journal of Community Psychology* that I found out how routinely many people respond to rejections with resubmissions. I doubt it occurred to my faculty at Michigan or my colleagues at NYU that this was a lacuna in my training, although I suspect that men who are socialized in other ways to be more assertive may require less explicit instruction here. If there is wisdom in this essay to impart to younger scholars, it is not to roll over and play dead when an article or grant is not greeted with enthusiasm the first time out.

All that aside, New York and NYU were wonderful places to be a community psychologist. Unlike many smaller communities dominated by universities, where many potential community collaborators have been soured by experiences with irresponsible researchers, in New York, most organizations are open to research. When I moved to NYU, I started working on staff stress or burnout in human service agencies and individual, group (social support) and agency (more structural) coping strategies. I chose to work with residential programs for youths, because I knew something about the challenges staff faced from the Youth Home Development Project. Within months I had collaborative relationships with more agencies in New York than existed in Michigan's Lower Peninsula. Similarly, when I later applied the same paradigm to the situation of working parents, looking at flexible job schedules as a form of organizational coping, I quickly developed relationships with a set of insurance companies and a set of state agencies, each of which had similar within-set personnel policies but different within-set policies on flexible scheduling. Work on child care involved collaborations around the country brokered by Ellen Galinsky at Families and Work Institute.

I was lucky to spend a year amidst sociologists and political scientists as a fellow at the Russell Sage Foundation, where I learned that I am, in fact, a psychologist. After explaining to psychologists why situations matter, I had to explain to sociologists why individual well-being was important, and why psychological constructs they found superfluous (such as "needs") might in fact have some explanatory power.

Policy makers in New York actually request input from researchers, and have been remarkably cooperative in allowing or even soliciting rigorous studies of interactions between poor people and the systems that affect them. A longitudinal study of homeless and housed poor families was initiated by the city agency charged with homelessness, and led to a wonderful collaboration with Beth Weitzman and Jim Knickman of NYU's Wagner School of Public Service. More recently I have collaborated with innovative intervention programs on experimental studies of approaches to housing individuals with serious mental illnesses and families. Pathways to Housing, a "housing first" program that offers individuals with mental illness and often substance problems their own apartments, directly from the street, with services under their control, was founded and is directed by an NYU graduate, Sam Tsemberis. The program houses individuals faster and longer than programs that use housing as leverage to get individuals into treatment, but which leave many on the streets (Tsemberis, Moran, Shinn, Asmussen, & Shern, 2003). Unfortunately, homelessness is a growth industry in New York, allowing for studies that could not easily be done elsewhere. A recent study in the welfare system, in collaboration with the state- funded Nathan Kline Institute for mental health research, grew out of the City's concerns that women with mental health problems might have troubles satisfying the requirements of the system and moving to paid employment. A study requested by and done in collaboration with the New York City Department of Health examined the extent to which health departments serving large cities around the country use behavioral and social sciences in their work. Even collaborations that did not come to fruition, such as one invited by UNICEF to study job and family stressors experienced by the international civil service got far enough to provide rich learning experiences for students and for me. It's hard to imagine another city anywhere with equivalent opportunities.

I have also been blessed with wonderful colleagues and students from whom I have learned a great deal. Stan Lehmann kept me from taking myself too seriously. Barbara Felton was a wonderful colleague and collaborator. As a graduate student I had written my "prelim" (comprehensive) paper on similarities between deinstitutionalization in the mental health and criminal justice system. That paper was best consigned to recycling, but Felton added aging, and helped develop the idea into a special issue of the *Journal of Social Issues* (Shinn & Felton, 1981). Bringing Bruce Rapkin and Ed Seidman into the program was more like merging two programs than incorporating new faculty–I got some of the intellectual excitement of moving to another university while staying put. Rapkin and I collaborated on a chapter for the *Handbook of Community Psychology* (Shinn & Rapkin, 2000), and Seidman has been both an architect of the present form of the program and an intellectual guide to more transactional thinking. Diane Hughes brought rigorous theoretical approaches to race and racism and their relationship to processes such as job stress and racial socialization. Andrew Fuligni examined how immigrants handled the challenges of adolescence. Most recently, Hiro Yoshikawa has done brilliant work on welfare and other policies affecting poor children and on prevention of HIV. Dave Chavis, Jane Knitzer and Tony D'Augelli, as visiting faculty, brought unique insights about activism, policy, and gay and lesbian issues and family theory. All have contributed over the years to an amazingly vibrant and varied intellectual climate for a small program that has never numbered more than five faculty.

Combining Work and Family

When I married in 1981, I acquired three children, the youngest of whom, Ari, came to live with us for high school in 1984. We had two more children, the first in October, 1981. The Dean had promulgated a reasonably enlightened maternity policy–a semester's relief from teaching. Dan was a one-day-old low-birth-weight baby in the neonatal ICU when the department chair called me at the hospital to ask whether I wanted to come up early for promotion to Associate Professor. If so, I needed to have my materials ready by the end of the week (I declined). My second pregnancy was carefully planned, but conceived soon before Stan Lehmann entered the hospital with a terminal illness. Barbara Felton was on leave, and the only other faculty member at the time was a visitor. David Chavis was wonderful in helping to hold the program together, but students were understandably anxious, and I was back in the office with Marc three days after his birth in April, 1986. We had a new chair who was very supportive, and allowed me to teach my graduate course double-time in the first two months of the semester. (Our central administration had rescinded the maternity policy, which took our Women's Faculty Caucus many years to reinstate, and I couldn't desert the program in any case).

As these anecdotes suggest, combining work and family has sometimes been stressful, but well worth it. In addition to being a joy, the kids have helped me to keep perspective. One day when in day care, Dan queried my unusually formal clothing. He listened with a small child's solemnity when I explained that I wanted to look my best for an important presentation, then asked, puzzled, "But whose clothes are they?" Later, when I was elected president of Division 27 (now the Society for Community Research and Action) he pointed out that I was now in charge of two things. "Two?," I inquired. "The book fair, and . . . what was that other thing?"

All five children are activists (thankfully none rebelled by becoming Republicans), but are kinder about their parents' shortcomings than I was. Rachel is a social worker who has worked on violence against women, Becca is a doctoral student in sociology, studying community-based organizations, and Ari is a union-side labor lawyer. Dan, a college student, has been active in several political organizations, and Marc heads his high school's Amnesty International chapter. They are all good feminists, although Marc likes to tweak me, e.g., by labeling the doll we gave to our oldest grandson an "action figure." Rachel followed our example by keeping her name and hyphenating her children's. Ari and his children took his wife's name.

NEXT STEPS

When I joined the NYU faculty, I never imagined that I would still be here nearly twenty-five years later. Like many a community psychologist just launching a career, I continue to wonder about the best ways to make use of my particular blend of talents, failings, and opportunities to promote goals I believe in. The paths I have taken have been governed by chance as well as choice. For example, I began studying homelessness because I could not walk by people on the street without attempting to do something. My children's urgent empathy also contributed. But I am a better researcher than advocate, so chose to get involved by doing research. My approach to that research, focusing on ecological circumstances as well as personal characteristics, and then on ecological interventions, grew out of the theoretical and empirical traditions of community psychology. I expect future paths to be guided in similar ways, although I am not sure where they will lead. This was intended to be an essay about formative influences on me. All I can be certain of is that I am not yet fully formed.

REFERENCES

Bowers, D. G. (1973). OD techniques and their results in 23 organizations: The Michigan ICL study. *Journal of Applied Behavioral Science, 9*, 21-43.

Douglas, M. (1966/1970). *Purity and danger: An analysis of concepts of pollution and taboo*. London: Penguin.

Goffman, E. (1961). *Asylums: Essays on the social situation of mental patients and other inmates*. New York: Anchor.

Horner, M. S. (1970). Femininity and successful achievement: A basic inconsistency. In J. M. Bardwick, E. Douvan, M. S. Horner, & D. Guttman, *Feminine personality and conflict* (pp. 45-74). Belmont, CA: Brooks/Cole.

Moos, R. H. (1973). Changing the social milieus of psychiatric treatment settings. *Journal of Applied Behavioral Science, 9*, 575-593.

Moos, R. H. (1974). *Evaluating treatment environments: A social ecological approach*. New York: John Wiley and Sons.

Sarason, S. B. (1974). *The psychological sense of community: Prospects for a community psychology*. San Francisco: Jossey Bass.

Shinn, M., & Felton, B.J. (Eds.) (1981). Institutions and alternatives [Special issue]. *Journal of Social Issues, 37*(3).

Shinn, M., & Rapkin, B.D. (2000). Cross-level analysis without cross-ups. In J. Rappaport & E. Seidman (Eds.), *Handbook of community psychology.* (pp. 669-695). New York: Kluwer Academic/Plenum.

Tsemberis, S., Moran, L.L., Shinn, M., Asmussen, S. M., & Shern, D. L. (2003). Consumer preference programs for homeless individuals with psychiatric disabilities: A drop-in center and a supported housing program. *American Journal of Community Psychology, 32*, 305-317.

Warren, R. B., & Warren, D. I. (1977). *The neighborhood organizer's handbook*. Notre Dame: University of Notre Dame Press.

Reflections on *Becoming* a Community Psychologist

Rhona S. Weinstein

University of California, Berkeley

SUMMARY. This narrative traces the roots of my development as a community psychologist just as the field was beginning, and my emerging interests in the dynamics of negative self-fulfilling prophecies as a source of educational inequality. Critical personal influences included being the child of immigrant parents living as a Jewish minority in French Quebec, developmental opportunities provided by a unique summer camp setting, and obstacles encountered as a woman aspiring to an academic career. My graduate training in clinical and community psychology took place both at McGill University (1967-69) and Yale University (1968-1973). I was greatly influenced by two significant mentors, the late M. Sam Rabinovitch and Seymour B. Sarason, as well as their visionary clinical settings, the McGill-Children's Hospital Learning Centre and the Yale Psycho-Educational Clinic, respectively. From both mentors, I developed a passion for understanding and creating social settings that enhance human development. My fascination with classrooms

---

Address correspondence to: Department of Psychology, 3210 Tolman Hall, #1650, University of California, Berkeley, CA 94720-1650.

The author is particularly grateful for the stimulating undergraduate course in the history of psychology taught by Steve Glickman, in which she recently participated.

[Haworth co-indexing entry note]: "Reflections on *Becoming* a Community Psychologist." Weinstein, Rhona S. Co-published simultaneously in *Journal of Prevention & Intervention in the Community* (The Haworth Press, Inc.) Vol. 28, No. 1/2, 2004, pp. 125-147; and: *Six Community Psychologists Tell Their Stories: History, Contexts, and Narrative* (eds: James G. Kelly, and Anna V. Song) The Haworth Press, Inc., 2004, pp. 125-147. Single or multiple copies of this article are available for a fee from The Haworth Document Delivery Service [1-800-HAWORTH, 9:00 a.m. - 5:00 p.m. (EST). E-mail address: docdelivery@haworthpress.com].

http://www.haworthpress.com/web/JPIC
© 2004 by The Haworth Press, Inc. All rights reserved.
Digital Object Identifier: 10.1300/J005v28n01_07

and schools has never abated in a stimulating career devoted to community research and action. *[Article copies available for a fee from The Haworth Document Delivery Service: 1-800-HAWORTH. E-mail address: <docdelivery@haworthpress.com> Website: <http://www.HaworthPress.com> © 2004 by The Haworth Press, Inc. All rights reserved.]*

KEYWORDS. Marginality, educational opportunity, serendipity, gender discrimination, social settings, development

I vividly remember the moment in the fall of 1967 when I discovered the field of community psychology. Then a first year clinical graduate student, I served as an intern at the McGill University-Montreal Children's Hospital Learning Centre under the supervision of Professor M. Sam Rabinovitch. Contrary to popular belief, Rabinovitch demonstrated that children with learning disabilities were indeed of normal intelligence and could learn when they were appropriately taught. Among my first clinical emergencies was a young boy with whom I had been working, who was rushed into the emergency room. Upon his return from school, he had thrown himself through the picture window of his living room, crying out that he was stupid. While he recovered from his injuries, I did not. I found myself mulling over this frightening event, searching for an explanation.

The young boy had received the best of clinical and educational services. He had been extensively tested, a program of specialized tutoring and psychological support was well underway, and he was, in fact, making progress in his reading skills. Yet this appeared not to be enough. I asked if I might visit this boy's classroom where I could observe his experiences in school. I came back immensely sobered, finding myself better able to stand in his shoes. I saw that the teaching strategies did not match the needs of this child as well as many others, but blame was attributed to the student. I saw features of the classroom environment that made failure a public and humiliating event. Knowing that under different conditions this boy could learn, I began to think about the elements of negative self-fulfilling prophecies, long before I came across the research literature.

In our next case conference, I talked about what needed to be done in collaboration with teachers so as to prevent such sad outcomes. Sam Rabinovitch had come prepared and he handed me a precious gift–a heavy blue book of 714 pages. *Psychology in Community Settings* had been published in 1966 and was written by Sarason, Levine, Goldenberg, Cherlin, and Bennett. I read it cover to cover, well into that night. The words and ideas therein still evoke the same passion in me as they did at the time. In the opening lines, Seymour Sarason and his colleagues wrote about the magnitude of this paradigm shift for *them*:

> This is a book about the origins and activities of the Psycho-Educational Clinic in the department of Psychology at Yale, a service, training, and research facility that represents a new departure for our department and a marked change in the thinking and practices of those of us involved in the Clinic. It is no exaggeration to say that our lives have been so changed that it is hard for us to remember clearly what we did before the Clinic's existence. (p. vii)

And so in this cherished book, I discovered the new field of community psychology and have never looked back.

This year marks three decades that I have spent as a faculty member at the University of California, Berkeley as a community psychologist within a clinical psychology program. I have memories of first showing my parents around the campus following my hire. And I remember my father's words, as we walked through the glorious rooms of Doe Memorial Library: "Are they really going to pay you to come here each day to read anything your heart desires?" For my father and for me, this opportunity to be a professor was of the highest order.

It is important to place myself historically in the field and in the times. My graduate training in clinical and community psychology took place both at McGill (1967-1969) and Yale (1968-1973). I am part of a second-wave of community psychologists, taught by the founders of the field and the early second-generation cohort, just beginning faculty careers. I was also a post World War II child, of the so-called baby boomer generation. My life crossed two countries (Canada and the United States), and was marked by the experiences of minority and immigrant status, the civil rights and women's movements, and affirmative action. These experiences have colored my worldview and ultimately framed my research and social action.

FAMILY BACKGROUND

I grew up as the only child of older immigrant parents, a 41 year-old mother and 51 year-old father. Born in 1895 in Romania, my father, Alex Strasberg, had emigrated with his family to Canada in 1910 to escape discrimination against Jews and seek better opportunities. Born in

1905 in Vienna, my mother, Lotte Lubetzky, emigrated alone to Canada in 1924 to join her aunt and uncle following the suicide of her father. Her unwavering efforts to obtain scarce visas enabled her to save some of her family from the death camps of the Nazis. Both parents came to Montreal to live in a ghetto-like Jewish community within the French-speaking province of Quebec. They lived as double minorities, English-speaking as well as Jewish. They were immensely grateful for greater opportunities but always alert for signs of discrimination.

Ours was a serious household for a young girl growing up as an only child. My father spoke often of how hard he worked to fulfill his dream of becoming a physician. He was the first in his family to obtain a college education and he supported his schooling by pressing trousers for a living. He was several times denied entry into McGill University because of a quota on Jewish admissions, but ultimately graduated with a medical degree in 1921. Reflective of his motivation, his yearbook entry reads, "For where he set his heart, he set his hand: To do the thing he willed–and bore it through" (author unknown). He fought to gain hospital privileges at institutions that discriminated against Jewish doctors. Perhaps not surprisingly, my father devoted much of his career as a practicing urologist to providing low-fee services to poor immigrant communities, especially in Montreal's Chinatown. I often accompanied him on house calls and hospital visits, waiting at the gate or in corridors. He would explain the procedures that needed to be done and tell me of the life problems of his patients. At a time when abortion was illegal, he helped women obtain safe ones from qualified physicians–social action on his part about which I was particularly proud. In his office, he kept a monkey's skull, and between patients, I would pull out its teeth, using his urological instruments.

Despite this early medical training, it was my father's observations of the poverty of his patients and his descriptions of what would be a better health care system that caught my young eye. He had a unique practice–leaving long spaces between appointments so that he could read philosophy and write poetry. These ways of working as well as our nightly game of reading the Encyclopedia Britannica prepared me well for academe. He would allow me to pick one of the volumes, open it at any page, and he would read it aloud. Best of all, I escaped doing the dishes each night. This meant that I came to independent life totally inept in the kitchen–a deficit that likely saved me for career pursuits.

My mother shared the same passion for education as did my father but her own hopes, if she had them, were thwarted. She read voraciously, especially in biography and politics, and was eager to discuss books with anyone who was a serious reader. The rented apartment and flats in which I grew up were lined with books. Her intellect was never appreciated by her family in the Vienna of the early 20th century–it was viewed as a sign of disrespect. With the loss of her father, immigration to Canada, and the need to send money home, work appeared to be her only option beyond high school. But she had greater hopes for me. Upon my birth, she devoted all her energies to raising me and to taking care of her elderly, ill mother who lived with us. She became a formidable president of the PTA in every one of the three elementary schools that I attended. [The school changes resulted from one move and from redistricting.] She made it possible for school libraries to be enriched and for after-school programs in art, drama, and music to be offered free of charge to all comers. I remember principals being afraid of her footsteps, knowing that she would demand more programs for children.

Among the influences on my development were my parents' friendships with two of my father's colleagues–one, a black professor of pharmacology from the Caribbean and the other, a Chinese doctor from Taiwan. In these relationships that endured all their adult years, I saw close-up what acts of discrimination do to human lives. I also learned to appreciate, indeed, relish cultural differences–a rare opportunity in the Jewish neighborhood in which I lived. I was fascinated by differences in foods and customs, and in art and clothing that made us unique in interesting ways. I was also the silent listener to my parents' monthly speaker group that lasted 40 years. With my father as one of the founders, this group of friends rotated homes to host invited speakers from different fields, as well to encourage animated discussions. Finally, I was privy to intense discussions by and about the writers and activists in my mother's family who participated in socialist causes. These interracial friendships, the discussions, and the power of the published word and social action, primed me toward community psychology.

NEIGHBORHOOD, SCHOOL, AND SUMMER CAMP

I lived in Montreal neighborhoods that were religiously and linguistically segregated. Two school systems existed at the time: Roman Catholic for the French and Protestant for the English. Under Quebec educational policies, Jews were classified as Protestant for the purposes of instruction. In a school with virtually 100 percent Jewish population, this meant beginning each day with the Lord's Prayer and Christian hymns as well as membership in the Christmas choir–an irony that did not go unnoticed by me even as a young child. One of the saddest by-products of this educational system was that I never had a personal relationship with a French Canadian. On the streets, I learned the kind of petty prejudices that festered on both sides: a common game was to guess whether the occupants of passing cars were English or French, by facial expression and dress. While I have memories of being called a dirty Jew, I have even more powerful memories of being called "poor" for living below Queen Mary Road. This was the dividing line between the so-called upper-and middle/lower-class Jewish community–between those who owned houses, joined country clubs, and had material wealth versus those who rented. Despite this segregated enclave, I often felt like a minority in the larger context of the anti-Semitism of Quebec, especially feared by two parents who had fled Europe. And even within my own group, I felt apart, given the different values of my parents.

My public school education was uninteresting although I worked hard and did well academically. My memories are of rules and memorization, and of rights and wrongs in facts as well as in people. In the first grade, I was regularly kept after school for being left-handed and forced to write with my right hand. I emerged with a confusing ambidexterity, which I blame for my poor coordination and scattered learning disabilities. I remember surprising teachers by failing to test well enough for gifted classes. I remember the tension and shame of ability groups and tracks–feeling the pressure to be placed higher and fearing demotion. In high school, I witnessed the banishment of my best friend from the highest Latin track into the lowest clerical track for speaking out against our teacher's public ridicule of the wrong answers of students. No action on the part of our entire class, her parents, or my parents could undo that demotion, which undermined her opportunity for university but did not destroy her resilient creativity.

Thankfully, I had one memorable and beloved teacher in 5th grade, Miss Alexander. For dramatic emphasis, she stood on her desk, her right hand placed inside her blouse on her heart, and she recited her favorite poems to the class. She inspired me to read literature and poetry and I basked in her enthusiasm. More than 10 years later, when my future husband (a medical intern) looked up at the patient in the hospital bed, Miss Alexander greeted him with "You're marrying my Rhona." She had seen the engagement picture in the newspaper.

But my real intellectual, artistic, and social awakening first occurred in summer camps, which I attended from the ages of 10 through 21, first as a camper and then as a counselor. At Pripstein's Camp in the Laurentian mountains outside Montreal, I found a sacred place–perhaps because of the values that permeated this setting and the interesting young adults who tended the children. Serendipitously, one such counselor was Edward Bennett, later to be a co-author with Sarason of *Psychology in Community Settings*, but more about that later.

Mr. Pripstein was a social worker, who with his wife, created a small world that was respectful, inclusive, stimulating, and supportive to children and youth. From gatherings at the flagpole, to reading and discussion groups, to the ways in which the arts and sports were taught, to the inclusion of children with special needs in each cabin, and to interventions made by engaging young adults who were themselves in the throes of career development, all served to create a climate of possibility, social consciousness, and community. It was here that I felt most myself–where I first read books in psychology, first developed a passion for nature, sculpture, drama, and folk music (Leonard Cohen was also counselor there, and he and Pete Seeger were my idols), and first entertained the idea that I might become a psychologist.

But as time went on, I realized that I wanted to be a psychologist of a different order. What fascinated me most were the values, norms, and what Sarason has called the behavioral as well as programmatic regularities of this and other camps. At the age of 10, I noticed that camps differed enormously from each other. This was evident in the color war games that were played when camps came together to compete in sports marathons. At Pripstein's, the participation of all and individual improvement were lauded whereas in many other camps, the focus was on winning at any cost. By observing these differences between camps and between the "self" I was aware that in different kinds of settings, I became a social ecologist and social engineer without knowing it. Once a counselor, I took great joy in creating settings and developing programs for children and youth, especially targeted toward bringing out the best in each individual.

Yet as I struggled with my future directions, I came upon conflicting messages–the encouragement to grow intellectually against the backdrop of what it meant to be a young woman in the Montreal Jewish community of the 1960's. It meant marriage at 21, coiffed and elegantly dressed looks, and a never-ending devotion to being a good daughter, wife, and mother at every moment. This way of living stifled and infuriated me, long before I even heard of the women's movement. I became determined never to depend on any man for my livelihood. Despite this early decision to have a career, the doing of it engendered conflict–but I am getting ahead of the story.

UNDERGRADUATE YEARS AT MCGILL

I had no doubt that I would go to university, although at the time, most students were commuters still living at home. It was a tense time awaiting the results of the high school leaving exams, but I had achieved the grades to be admitted to McGill University. Once there, I found myself isolated in large classes and unable to break into campus life.

I knew that gaining entry into a two-year honors program would greatly enrich my experience but the question of field had yet to be answered. I sampled philosophy which I loved but grew impatient with what I felt was the absence of a testable method of inquiry. I became enamored with anthropology, but found myself less interested in foreign cultures: I wanted to study local culture, which at that time was not fashionable. I loved sociology: I remember a census tract assignment where we documented the qualities of a particular neighborhood in detailed text and diagrams, but in the doing of it, I missed the study of individuals. Finally, I found my passion in psychology in the introductory course taught by Donald Olding Hebb, where he revealed with breathtaking clarity the nature of hypothesis testing in scientific experiments. Hebb used his textbook *An Introduction to Psychology* (1963). While his presentation seemed sparse at the start, Hebb's ideas about neural models and synapses, about intelligence, perception, and early learning simply exploded with excitement. I had read some psychology earlier, mostly Freud and Jung, but I had not been exposed to experimentation. I was hooked by the elegance of it.

Happily, I was admitted to the McGill honors program in psychology (1965-1967)–a challenging program that herded 25 students through two years of seminars as well as two independent research studies. These were immensely satisfying years since we were mentored closely by the faculty and were part of a wonderful cohort of students who supported each other. Hebb also taught us about our obligation to publish immediately, not lest we perish but rather to inform others about what was learned and how. The values that permeated the McGill Psychology Department at that time have become ingrained in how I train my own students.

My turn to clinical psychology came about, in part, as a result of the following incident. In repeating classical studies, my assignment was to conduct a retrograde amnesia experiment with rats: I taught them to run a maze, applied electric shock, and measured learning retention. Fortunately or unfortunately, I was afraid of the animals and technologically inept. I quivered when I picked up the rats. I failed to administer the shock appropriately, accidentally killing one rat and shocking another rat clear out of the apparatus. Hebb found me in tears chasing the runaway rat down the hall. Ordering me into his office, he sternly suggested that I might be happier in clinical psychology.

Ultimately I took his advice but for my research projects, I became fascinated with psycholinguistics, in particular, the role of syntactic structure in memory. I completed two studies that became my first publications, one with Albert Bregman and another with Sam Rabinovitch. I experimentally demonstrated that poor readers were less able than normal readers to make use of syntactic structure in learning a set of nonsense sentences, with and without embedded syntactic cues (Weinstein & Rabinovitch, 1971). The sentences that I had created for this latter study still ring in my ears (e.g., "When they sivoled the veg, they hanished zalfully"). In a recent graduate student qualifying examination some 30 years later, I had a good laugh to find a professor of education finish these nonsense sentences for me, aptly illustrating the enduring impact of publishing one's work. But despite my fascination with experimental psychology, I felt rather uneasy. I did not want to describe deficits. I wanted to fix them.

Psychology became my total focus during these college years, between 1963 and 1967. The furor of the 1960s was a U.S. phenomenon. Although I read about, indeed knew a few individuals who traveled to Washington and the South to participate in antiwar and civil rights demonstrations (one of my female classmates was killed during such a visit), I stayed on the sidelines, but envious of the protesters' convictions. Being Canadian at the time meant not being a player, not taking a stand, but keeping an inward focus on our own–although our own became more complicated as the separatist movement developed in Quebec. In those years, Canada was described as having an inferiority complex. Everything was viewed as better, more exciting, and bolder, south of the border. In hindsight, with greater understanding of the social and political policies of Canada, I have come to wonder at that perception.

Despite my apparent success in the honors program, I came up against the tyranny of standardized testing. The Miller Analogies Test was required for application to graduate programs in clinical psychology, although later research showed that the scores had no relevance for performance in the field. I was called in by two of my professors who ran the career service. I was told that I had received the lowest score ever recorded at McGill, I was not graduate student material, and I ought not to apply. I chose to ignore the advice, but their predictions about my admission chances were borne out, as I was refused entry at all eight American universities to which I had applied. Happily, I was accepted at two Canadian universities and ultimately chose McGill over York, because of its research emphasis. I later took great glee at informing one of the professors that her prediction was not confirmed. I had obtained my PhD from Yale, and had garnered a faculty position at Berkeley, despite her lack of faith in me.

MARRIAGE

I did marry at age 21 to Harvey Weinstein, a medical intern, whom I had been dating for about a year. On our first date, he proposed and I laughed. Perhaps I was worn out by his argument that if I did not marry him it was indeed my last chance, and also by my mother's support of his view. But I did rather impulsively accept his proposal during the second week of graduate school and we married by the end of the first semester. The implications, which I had not thought through at the time, were enormous. This decision unleashed years of complex negotiation as we each struggled to have the careers we wanted (with our decision-points wildly out of sync) and to live a balanced life together. It was far from easy but we eventually worked through it by taking turns. And each of us grew in the company of the other, now across 35 years of marriage. Among our gifts to each other was the daily supervision, as Harvey became a community psychologist through me, and I became a psychiatrist and then a public health physician working in human rights when he returned to school and changed fields. We are the best of friends and colleagues. Without his enduring intellectual and emotional support, I would not have pursued all that I did, nor in the ways that I did.

Perhaps our greatest collaboration has been the parenting of wonderful twin sons now grown; Jeremy, a political economist about to embark on his own academic career, and Joshua, an actor, vocalist, and writer. Family has been the center of our lives as has been the sharing of the inherent responsibilities. We became interchangeable parents, which was deeply satisfying. Being home for dinner was always a priority as was participating in the important events of our children's lives, even as adults. This meant keeping a tight lid on committees, conferences, and papers, in order to make room for these remarkable life experiences. In leaving Montreal behind, and in living more than 3000 miles away from aging parents, we lost whatever familial support might have been available as well as incurred the stress of multiple trips back to help with the inevitable illnesses. All told, we faced 20 years of coping with the Alzheimer's disease and senile dementia of three parents, while raising our sons. We were indeed the "sandwiched" generation. The balancing act of dual careers and family life was made possible only by giving up something in each domain. But looking back, this pathway not only enriched our lives but also the nature of our work. I understand children and schools better having been a parent, and I have learned much about the health system and community supports in pursuing the care of my parents–all of which came to shape my understanding of community psychology.

GRADUATE STUDY AT McGILL

Graduate study at McGill in 1967-1968 was a riveting enterprise. Hebb set the tone for the department with the first year graduate seminar. It was held weekly, spanned two semesters, and all faculty and graduate students were required and, indeed, did attend. The first year students made three presentations on topics they picked out of a hat: for 15, 10, and 5 minutes, respectively, to be timed by Hebb's stopwatch. The goal was to critically integrate the research literature and point to promising new directions for research, in increasingly succinct ways. I remember my first topic (psychophysics) and how my legs shook when I spoke. This seminar provided us with a unified view of psychology and held us accountable for brief professional presentations (even outside our own specialty areas) from which faculty might learn. This experience cemented my interest in each part of the field as well as conveyed that clinical psychology, the poor applied cousin in so many programs, was indeed a scientific enterprise.

The highlight was Sam Rabinovitch, who supervised my research as well as my clinical work at the Learning Centre. I can still picture Sam, with a pipe in his mouth, looking me straight in the eye, and thoughtfully answering my questions. Some 10 years later in 1977, Dr. Sam (as he was called by the children), died while only in his forties, with so much yet to accomplish. The Learning Centre that Sam and others, such as Margie Golick, created in 1960 was an unusual clinical setting. Wiener and Siegel (1992) wrote that "the Learning Centre was the major influence on professional practice with children with learning disabilities in Canada and its basic philosophy and practice would even now be considered to be progressive" (p. 342). The key words that they used to describe the work are "teaching, whole child, and collaborative consultation" (p. 343). What Sam and others did was to tie assessment to intervention in the treatment of children with learning disabilities. Sam used the testing situation to alter inquiry so that he could demonstrate the optimal conditions under which children can demonstrate their knowledge and learn best. This was assessment for a different purpose and children emerged from the experience with the knowledge of what they could accomplish and how they could be helped to do even more. Also central to the mission of the Centre was the mandate that all were accountable for good teaching–the psychologists as well as the teachers.

Only later did I see the connections between the visions of Sam and of Seymour and how they have in interwoven ways influenced my own research and practice as a community psychologist. I later discovered that Sam made a film with Robert Rosenthal in 1971 called "What Teacher Expects" which illustrates self-fulfilling prophecies in an experimental context with teachers and students working together. I later discovered that Seymour was sharply critical of our test-giving society. As a result of his work with individuals diagnosed with mental retardation at Southbury Training School in the early 1940s, he re-envisioned assessment as demonstrating the capacity to learn. In his autobiography (1988), Sarason wrote "What I failed to grasp at Southbury . . . was to be viewed as smart or unintelligent in America was indeed fateful for one's existence. . . . I knew about the self-fulfilling prophecy long before it became a subject of psychological study" (p. 151, 154).

I found the work at the Learning Centre immensely satisfying but all this was to come to a quick end, given my decision to marry. Following news of my engagement, I was called into the department chairman's office and asked for my resignation in order to free up a space for a more committed student, undoubtedly male. I refused, more shamed than angered, as I was yet unaware of the women's movement. But this action fueled the rage of Sam Rabinovitch who chastised the chairman for his intervention.

Greater trouble was to come in the mismatch between my new husband's career plans and my own. For a complicated set of reasons, he was desperate to leave Montreal for his psychiatry training (Weinstein, 1990). In the first semester of graduate school, just weeks before my wedding, I applied for a second time to American schools so that we might both find opportunities in the same city. I was again rejected. My husband chose Yale University and Sam Rabinovitch made a brave plea but to no avail in a telephone call to the chairman of the Psychology Department at Yale. My husband made a similar but failed plea for help from the Department of Psychiatry. "We have so many Yale wives . . . " is the answer I remember. Thus, I faced the possibility that I might not become the psychologist I wanted to be.

It was to be Sam Rabinovitch's feminist thinking and my summer camp connections that saved my professional life. Revolutionary in 1968, his suggestion was that I become a commuter–I would remain in the clinical program at McGill but I would move with my husband to Yale. Sam won approval for this plan from the faculty despite my only one year of full residency in the program. Happily, this generous offer gave me an institutional home and the opportunity to continue my research, take qualifying examinations, and seek further educational opportunities in New Haven. Serendipitously, it was around this time that Sam handed me *Psychology in Community Settings*, and planted the seed that I work at the Yale Psycho-Educational Clinic. Upon calling Professor Sarason, I was told that he was not making appointments and the door remained closed. But serendipitously again, the book co-author's name, Edward Bennett, evoked memories of Eddie, the waterfront director at Pripstein's camp. I wondered if they were one and the same. Telephone calls to all the Bennetts in the Montreal telephone book put me in touch with Ed's proud parents and landed me his telephone number in New Haven. And it was Ed who helped me find an apartment in New Haven, and most importantly, obtained a precious appointment with Seymour Sarason.

I did not know that Seymour and Sam were kindred spirits not only in their intellectual interests but also in their passion for overturning the constraints of bureaucratic systems. I still remember opening the door of 295 Crown Street, the crumbling but gracious three-story brownstone that housed the Yale Psycho-Educational Clinic. On the right was the office of Anita Miller (the formidable yet loving force that held the Clinic together), with a reception area, in which I was welcomed. "Professor Sarason," she said, "Your appointment is here." My excitement about *Psychology in Community Settings* did not seem enough to engage him. My plight at being rejected from the Psychology department at Yale and my offer to work for free was greeted with a Seymourian sigh "I am sorry but I have nothing to offer you." I found myself sobbing that I simply had to work with him or I could not survive. He shifted in his chair and literally awoke with a plan. Since I was a continuing graduate student at McGill, he would accept me as a paid intern at the Clinic, which could count toward my requirements at McGill. This was accomplished without a look at test scores, transcripts, or letters of recommendation. When I reapplied to the Yale clinical program after a semester of work at the Clinic, I was accepted. Finally, I was fully launched!

GRADUATE STUDY AT YALE

On the first Monday in September 1968, at the age of 22, I appeared at the Yale Psycho-Educational Clinic as a psychology intern, much to the surprise of the faculty and fellow interns. It was also Dick Reppucci's first day as a new faculty member and he was later to become my dissertation advisor. Words cannot do justice to the intellectual climate of the Clinic and to the bit of heaven it provided me for four years (1968-1972). I have never stopped missing this most formative setting for my intellectual development. Murray Levine, who had left before I arrived, still carries the key to the building on his key chain. In a second, I can place myself back there–the musty smell of an aging building, the deli lunches that we shared in the clinic kitchen, the sound of footsteps running up three flights of stairs to our cherished offices, the excited cacophony of voices that came from the conference room where we argued and laughed together every Friday, and the beloved people. In my era, this included fellow graduate students (Terry Saunders, Verne MacArthur, Brian Sarata, Andrew Schwebel, Lee Wilkinson, and Cary Cherniss), faculty (Seymour Sarason, Ira Goldenberg, Fran Kaplan Grossman, Dick Reppucci, and Ed Trickett), and school psychologist (Kate McGraw). Among us were four graduates of Pripstein's Camp (Ed Bennett, Penny Rhodes, Sonny Cytrynbaum, and myself).

Seymour had launched the Clinic in 1962 with these bold plans spelled out in his autobiography (1988):

> that it be a place from which to go out, not come into; that the goals be to understand community settings and how to change them; that the priority be schools (to pay homage to Lightner Witmer who started the first Psychology Clinic in 1896 for educational problems); and that attention be paid to creating a setting that would supportively engage a diversity of people doing what everyone did (no differentiated staffing) but with limited resources so as to avoid the influence of funding. If we could not create the conditions in which we could learn, change, and grow, how could we help others to do it? (Sarason, 1988, p. 360)

Given these goals, the structure for my internship year was not surprising. That first Monday morning, we were each given four envelopes for the settings in which we would be working (for me: an inner-city day care center, an inner-city residential center for juvenile offenders, and two rural elementary schools). We were to return to the Clinic on Fridays for meetings and supervision. It was not easy to leave the clinic that day and set out into the community. I remember asking what will we do, how can we introduce ourselves, what do the directors and principals think we are there for? And I recall Seymour's answer: "learn about the problems they deal with, see what psychology has to offer, and bring your observations back to the Clinic." The boldness of this approach at that time stunned us–a group of whites venturing out into African American communities for some of our placements. For myself, in these early days in New Haven, I was reeling from culture shock but the prior experiences from which I drew great strength were my father's practice in Montreal's Chinatown and my parents' interracial friendships.

The climate at the Friday meetings was electric in its energy. At Seymour's behest, everyone had to sit around the conference table and be seen. Seymour's musings, his questions, turned everything on its side. Just when you thought you had a handle on a problem, Seymour would probe and you would instantly see your blinders. We, the students, would talk about how we could get ahead of him so we would not be surprised by his insights. Yet we could never get ahead. Seymour's insights always surprised, but once said, seemed obvious to all.

I thrived in this world where all of us shared an interest in social settings, their impact on human behavior, and social change. My eyes were opened to the possibility of preventive intervention at a systems level. My early interests in anthropology and sociology were finally integrated with psychology, and with applied goals–not only to describe and fix but also to prevent and promote. I learned enormously from Dick Reppucci about the principles of institutional change (Reppucci, 1973) and from Ed Trickett about the power of ecological theory (Trickett & Todd, 1972). And I became simply fascinated by school settings. While Seymour focused on the universals of schooling, I found myself attuned to the differential experiences within schools dependent upon who you are–the special plight of children who were different in any way from the norm. This interest, fueled by my observations in schools and by the insights of both Rabinovitch and Sarason, led me to study an individual, social, institutional, and societal influence process called the self-fulfilling prophecy–an inquiry that became a lifelong passion (Weinstein, 2002b).

There was also the broader world of the Yale Psychology Department. Once accepted into the program, it became my world, too, and the transition between department and the clinic was never easy. Indeed, Seymour decided to close the Psycho-Educational Clinic in 1972 after a decade in operation because Yale was not a place in which the young faculty could be tenured. As he said: "I started the clinic to start a family, not to become the sole source of continuity there" (Sarason, 1988, p. 375). Given Yale's pyramidal tenure structure, few achieved tenure, but the rift ran even deeper–the work of those in the Psycho-Educational tradition (naturalistic observation and social action at a setting level) did not fit the mold of mainstream psychology as represented in the department. This was also true for clinical psychology, as most of our teaching faculty were housed in Psychiatry. As Clinic interns, we were not immune to these tensions. Yet, we had to pass the departmental courses and requirements. Yale, at that time, was intensely competitive. First year course performance was used as a sorting mechanism–it was commonly said "Look to your left, look to your right. At least one of you won't be around next year." There was much talk about "brilliant" ideas, and we graduate students wondered how one could produce a "brilliant" idea.

Despite this difficult climate, there were many memorable training experiences. Particularly pivotal to my development was the opportunity to meet with William Kessen in an informal weekly seminar that ran for two years where a precious few of us (Carol Dweck, Allison Clarke Stewart, David Kuttner, and myself) read and talked about child development in the context of schooling. My dissertation study entitled "Reading Groups and Teacher-Child Interaction in the First-Grade Classroom" was guided by Dick Reppucci (as chair), Seymour Sarason, and Claude Buxton, and proved to be an immensely challenging adventure (Weinstein, 1976). In order to frame my research questions, I needed to reconcile what I observed in the real world of schools, with conceptual definitions of self-fulfilling prophecies that arose from sociology (Merton, 1948), verification that came from experiments in social psychology (Rosenthal & Jacobson, 1968), and information about underlying mechanisms that drew from structured and quantitative observation systems (Brophy & Good, 1970) as well as ethnographic field notes (Rist, 1970). I had to interweave elegance in design and measurement with the capacity to capture real world phenomenon–an interdisciplinary struggle that has persisted throughout my career. At Ed Trickett's suggestion, I read Jim Kelly's seminal chapter (1969) entitled "Naturalistic Observations in Contrasting Social Environments" and felt lucky to discover a community psychologist who was engaged in precisely that struggle. I was also blessed to have Dick Reppucci as the "pruner" of my tree since he was able to help shape the study into a manageable set of questions.

The clinical training we received was exceptional, although I was to find that my heart remained firmly with community psychology. Here, I saw the best of community mental health in the intensive and multidisciplinary team approach to working with adolescents facing their first psychotic break with the goal of quickly reintegrating them back into the community and preventing relapse. Here, I also saw the limits of psychodynamic thinking when I, as an intern, was asked to interpret my patient's lateness to the therapeutic hour as resistance whereas my own inquiry had revealed a single mother struggling with child care and public transportation in order to obtain help for herself. Just beyond the modern and clean walls of the Connecticut Mental Health Center lay enormous poverty, community anger, and a growing tide of unrest. I found it increasingly difficult to stay inside the psyches of individuals.

Outside my training walls in the larger world of New Haven, all was not well. I arrived the year prior to the admission of women to an all-male undergraduates college. I remember the sting of being left at the door of a pub and refused entry because I was a woman. Dick valiantly led my fellow male interns out the door in loud protest. When I attempted to rent our first apartment in New Haven without my husband present, I was denied every apartment for which I applied. It was a local who had to explain the discrimination at hand–implicit practices not to rent to African Americans. Without being able to see my husband, no landlord wished to take a chance.

The late 1960s was a time of enormous gaps between town and gown, rising unemployment and crime, the stirring hopes of the War on Poverty and the great disappointment in what it could not accomplish, the race riots on the New Haven Green, and protests against the Vietnam War. My husband and I played a role in helping conscientious objectors, we participated in T-groups, I joined women's groups, and bit by bit, we became more politically aware and active–more American, it appeared to us at the time. These experiences helped me reject the interpretation of my psychotherapist (personal therapy was strongly advised by the clinical program): that my wish to become a professor reflected my resistance to femininity and motherhood. In all of this turmoil, the Yale

Psycho-Educational Clinic provided a stable anchor–warm social relationships that crossed faculty-student lines and the capacity to sing the songs of communities. My joy in folk music blossomed at Yale, in part due to the talents of Ed Trickett and his determination to sing and profess at the same time.

A transition time was again approaching–never easy for dual career couples. My husband had completed his psychiatry training but I was not yet finished with my PhD. The compromise was that he would take a job at the University of Connecticut Medical School so that I would have more time at Yale. The next choice point would be his, but in a city that would be large enough to offer me opportunities, and San Francisco it was. We adopted a five-year plan; that is, if one partner was not happy, we would move again. I was writing my dissertation and during this time, I hoped that an academic job might turn up in the Bay area. If not, I planned to apply for a postdoctoral fellowship. And turn up it did–a coveted position in clinical psychology at Berkeley. But surprisingly, I did not learn of the opening until after the deadline had passed and applicants had been interviewed, and I learned of the position from a psychologist friend, not from Yale. Although the department informed students of job postings, my name was not on the list. Upon inquiring, I heard these rumblings: I had already left and followed my husband; I was planning a family and likely not a good bet for an academic job. Despite the difficult climate and the rarity of women faculty role models, the Yale Psychology Department produced a startling number of female academics during this era (among them, Allison Clarke Stewart, Carol Dweck, Shelley Taylor, Ellen Langer, Jeanne Marecek, and myself).

THE BERKELEY YEARS

In the archived words of Philip Cowan (1973): "Rhona Weinstein, having completed the total set of rituals at Yale, joins the full-time faculty, to develop a community psychology approach to clinical problems." It was serendipity again. The job description written in the fall of 1972 called for a clinical/community psychologist interested in schools and consultation. Today, it would not be possible to apply after a deadline, but this was the second year of affirmative action for women and ethnic minorities at Berkeley. Phil Cowan, head of the search committee and a fellow Canadian, had visited the Psycho-Educational Clinic and returned impressed. As a consultant to elementary schools, he viewed children's learning problems as resulting from a child-environment mismatch (Cowan, 1970). Sheldon Korchin, the director of the clinical program and an old friend of Seymour, was teaching an undergraduate course in community psychology, and in his 1976 textbook *Modern Clinical Psychology*, he included a chapter on the field. I later discovered that Jean Walker MacFarlane, a 1922 graduate of Berkeley's Psychology Department and early faculty member, had written a prescient paper in 1950 entitled "The Training of Psychologists for the Community Mental Health Service Field" for the *Journal of Clinical Psychology*. An interest in community psychology was already evident at Berkeley.

I gave two talks during my visit: "Membership in a Reading Group: A Significant Event in Classroom Life" and "The Introduction of Change: An Unfinished Case History." I remember enjoying the talks because the faculty shared memories of school experiences, their own and those of their children. The question period was richly interesting and not aggressive–a feature of Berkeley's development-focused achievement culture. And it was the biological psychologists who had wonderful questions, reminding me of McGill and of a commitment to a unified psychology. Once hired, I became the third faculty member in this small clinical psychology program and the third woman in a department of 40 members. On the campus, women constituted 3% of the 1500 faculty as compared to 22% today; all of us could fit in one small room. By becoming pregnant in my second year, I became the first woman faculty in the department to give birth, at a time when there was not yet a maternity leave in place.

I will touch on three aspects of these early years at Berkeley that especially shaped my journey of "becoming" a community psychologist. These included the need to create support; the particular values of this host setting; and obstacles that I faced as a female–all of which came to influence my work.

Despite a broad welcome, Berkeley's Psychology Department was a bit like Noah's ark–hiring one (not two) of each type of psychologist. And I remained as the only "wholly" community psychologist in a clinical program–an especially difficult transition after the Yale Psycho-Educational Clinic. To ease this transition, I invited Jim Kelly, whom I had wanted to meet, to visit during my first year on the faculty. It was Jim's advice that proved critical, when he told me that social networks had to be created and he showed me how. He also connected me to Lonnie Snowden and Ricardo Munoz, both of whom later moved to the Bay Area. We began a Community Psychology Interest Group, both big and small. As a threesome, we became a support group for each other, with monthly dinners over 10 years to help refine our work and move up the academic ladder. It was especially instructive to my own growth that we represented the perspectives of a woman, an African American, and a Latino.

I also took continuing education courses at the American Psychological Association meetings, including George Albee's course on prevention. I attended Robert Reiff's lively conference on social change at the Sterling Center (New York) in April 1975, where I first met Ed Seidman, Josh Holahan, and Lonnie Snowden, among others. Bob Reiff was not happy to greet a pregnant community psychologist in such a rural area, when unbeknownst to me it was just six weeks prior to my delivery of twins. This reality led to my missing the Austin conference on the training of community psychologists. Both national and local support proved pivotal in keeping my community perspective alive in an environment in which I sometimes found myself with a minority view.

The values of Berkeley and the University of California system, and the ethnic diversity of the state shaped my work in profound ways. The achievement culture of the system focused attention on faculty governance, equity of opportunity, the substance (not quantity) of scholarship, and the teaching enterprise–development-focused beliefs about which I have recently written (Weinstein, 2002b). This culture socialized me to be responsive to the intellectual concerns of other faculty (an interdependence of sort) so that my choices in research, teaching, and social action, had to be explained through the different disciplinary lenses of others. Although I arrived with such interdisciplinary leanings, Berkeley nurtured them further. The application of a developmental and social-cognitive approach to studying children's understanding of the dynamics of self-fulfilling prophecies and the exploration of mediating mechanisms in such effects no doubt made this research more understandable within a mainstream psychology and in my tenure review. Phil Cowan was a tremendous influence in articulating our joint commitment to the study of mechanisms–operative in descriptive as well as intervention studies. Within the clinical program, all faculty supervised intervention–a core value that united us around a common vision, and thus made room for preventive intervention. Our program also made a very early commitment to the study of ethnic minority mental health (Jones & Korchin, 1982) and the training of ethnic minority psychologists, in the context of the growing ethnic diversity of California and the campus. My own work increasingly turned toward the educational experiences of ethnic minority students and to teaching community psychology from an American Cultures perspective.

While all the above were positive influences, mounting a community psychology track within a clinical program with one mainstay faculty member proved to be a tremendous challenge. This forced me to reach and teach broadly, to supervise community intervention across diverse systems and communities, and to engage the initiative of students, both undergraduate and graduate in designing their own community intervention research projects. While the pressures were enormous, as detailed in a particularly cathartic paper of mine (Weinstein, 1981), there were tremendous opportunities gained by the self-initiated work of our students. A hallmark of my years at Berkeley has been working with cohorts of superb students who have made a place for themselves in community psychology or became a different kind of clinical or school psychologist as a result of these experiences.

Finally, the obstacles that women faced in carving a career impacted my work as well. Becoming pregnant in my second year on the faculty was similar to becoming engaged during my first semester of graduate school—both were threats to the male-dominated environments in which I worked. I received three requests for my resignation, extra teaching assignments to make clear my commitment, comments that I should be at home taking care of my children, and a dismal mid-career review with the advice that I might think of leaving prior to the tenure review. On the other hand, I received tremendous support from both male and female colleagues (especially the late Jeanne H. Block)—all said that I could make tenure and they would help me. Most importantly, they re-attributed my difficulties away from personal failure to the institutional structure that was far from welcoming to women. I learned about the institutional constraints upon women in the academy and in society at large. I ultimately saw connections between our societal view of race, gender, and special need and the underestimation of the human potential to grow—parallel processes that impacted faculty as well as first graders. Among my proudest accomplishment was participating in the creation of new policy at Berkeley—particularly, the extension of time to tenure for both male and female faculty who have young children and the creation of a document *Advancement and Promotion of Junior Faculty at U.C. Berkeley*. This survival manual, first written in 1981 by Susan Ervin Tripp and myself, was passed along the underground as an implicit curriculum. It is now posted on the university website, reflective of true social change.

CONCLUSION

I have never lost my fascination with the impact of schools on children's development and specifically the role of negative self-fulfilling prophecies–both to understand their dynamics and also to reduce their impact through systemic changes in classrooms, schools, and society. These social influence processes are at the heart of educational inequality–a silent burden unfairly carried by children who are poor, ethnic minority, speak a different language, have special needs, and learn in different ways (Weinstein, 2002a). My work has made room for children's perspectives as well as for an ecological understanding of the individual and contextual features that magnify or diminish the negative impact of such expectancy processes on children's lives (Weinstein, 2002b).

In the Psychology Department at McGill University, I first learned about the beauty of hypothesis testing in science. There, Sam Rabinovitch taught me about how teaching environments can better meet children's needs and help them fulfill their potential. Seymour Sarason and the Yale Psycho-Educational Clinic family broadened my disciplinary framework by orienting me to person and problem, as nested in the complex world of social settings. There, my understanding of the culture of schools and the processes of change was richly deepened. My life experience made me sensitive to the social influence processes of institutions and society that undermine opportunities for optimal development, especially for those who appear different to the mainstream culture. Despite the doors I found closed to me as a female and a low test-scorer, I am delighted that in my world, there were far more individuals, many white male community psychologists at heart, who relished opening doors to the fascinating questions that lay within our field of interest.

REFERENCES

Brophy, J. E., & Good, T. L. (1970). Teachers' communication of differential expectations for children's classroom performance: Some behavioral data. *Journal of Educational Psychology, 61,* 365-374.

Cowan, P. A. (1970). The nature of psycho-educational diagnosis. In D. B. Carter (Ed.). *Interdisciplinary approaches to learning disorders.* Philadelphia, PA: Chilton.

Hebb, D. O. (1963). *A textbook of psychology.* (2nd ed.) Philadelphia, PA: W. B. Saunders.

Jones, E. E., & Korchin, S. J. (1982). *Minority mental health.* New York: Praeger.

Kelly, J. G. (1969). Naturalistic observations in contrasting social environments. In E. P. Willems & H. L. Raush (Eds.), *Naturalistic viewpoints in psychological research*. New York: Holt, Rinehart, and Winston.

Korchin, S. J. (1976). *Modern clinical psychology*. New York: Basic Books.

MacFarlane, J. W. (1950). The training of psychologists for the community mental health service field. *Journal of Clinical Psychology, 6*, 128-132.

Merton, R. K. (1948). The self-fulfilling prophecy. *Antioch Review, 8*, 193-210.

Reppucci, N. D. (1973). The social psychology of institutional change: General principles for intervention. *American Journal of Community Psychology, 1*, 330-341.

Rist, R. (1970). Student social class and teacher expectations: The self-fulfilling prophecy in ghetto education. *Harvard Educational Review, 40*, 411-451.

Rosenthal, R. & Jacobson, L. (1968). *Pygmalion in the classroom: Teacher expectation and pupils' intellectual development*. New York: Holt, Rinehart, and Winston.

Sarason, S. B. (1988). *The making of an American psychologist: An autobiography*. San Francisco, CA: Jossey-Bass.

Sarason, S. B., Levine, M., Goldenberg, I. I., Cherlin, D. L., & Bennet, E. M. (1966). *Psychology in community settings: Clinical, educational, vocational, social aspects*. New York: John Wiley & Sons.

Trickett, E. J., & Todd, D. M. (1972). The high school culture: An ecological perspective. *Theory into Practice, 11*, 28-37.

Weinstein, H. M. (1990). *Psychiatry and the CIA: Victims of mind control*. Washington, D. C.: American Psychiatric Press.

Weinstein, R. S. (1976). Reading group membership in first grade: Teacher behaviors and pupil experience over time. *Journal of Educational Psychology, 71*, 103-116.

Weinstein, R. S. (1981). Teaching community intervention in a clinical program: Reflections in the themes of supervision. *American Journal of Community Psychology, 9*, 681-696.

Weinstein, R. S. (2002a). Overcoming inequality in schooling: A call to action for community psychology. *American Journal of Community Psychology, 30*, 21-42.

Weinstein, R. S. (2002b). *Reaching higher: The power of expectations in schooling*. Cambridge, MA: Harvard University Press.

Weinstein, R. S., & Rabinovitch, M. S. (1971). Sentence structure and retention in good and poor readers. *Journal of Educational Psychology, 62*, 25-30.

Wiener, J., & Siegel, L. S. (1992). A Canadian perspective on learning disabilities. *Journal of Learning Disabilities, 25*, 340-350.

Memories

Henrika Kuklick

University of Pennsylvania

KEYWORDS. Discipline formation, occupational identity, generational perspectives, marginality

What sorts of problems does a scholar of the history and sociology of science routinely confront when she uses autobiographies as sources? She knows that individuals' memories are of highly variable quality. Some are reliable, while others betray extravagantly revisionist tendencies–in all manner of ways and for all manner of reasons. How can she determine whom to trust? She assumes that she should believe individuals' recollections when they are echoed by others, yet she may fear that she is confronting collective delusion when she hears many sources speaking in unison.

Consider the autobiographies of the first generation of persons trained in community psychology–the disciples of those who founded the sub-field. The autobiographies exhibit substantial agreement about the initial conceptualization and academic organization of community psychology. It was in some measure conceived in opposition to clinical

---

Henrika Kuklick is affiliated with the Department of History and Sociology of Science, University of Pennsylvania, Philadelphia, PA 19104-6304 (E-mail: hkuklick@sas.upenn.edu).

[Haworth co-indexing entry note]: "Memories." Kuklick, Henrika. Co-published simultaneously in *Journal of Prevention & Intervention in the Community* (The Haworth Press, Inc.) Vol. 28, No. 1/2, 2004, pp. 149-152; and: *Six Community Psychologists Tell Their Stories: History, Contexts, and Narrative* (eds: James G. Kelly, and Anna V. Song) The Haworth Press, Inc., 2004, pp. 149-152. Single or multiple copies of this article are available for a fee from The Haworth Document Delivery Service [1-800-HAWORTH, 9:00 a.m. - 5:00 p.m. (EST). E-mail address: docdelivery@haworthpress.com].

http://www.haworthpress.com/web/JPIC
© 2004 by The Haworth Press, Inc. All rights reserved.
Digital Object Identifier: 10.1300/J005v28n01_08

psychology, to therapeutic approaches that ignored the importance of social circumstances in the creation of individuals' problems. And such figures as Seymour Sarason, Emory Cowen, and James Kelly played vital roles in carving out a niche for the sub-field within psychology, a niche defined by both an intellectual rationale and development of specific spheres of professional practice.

Yet, the very consistency that reassures the reader that the autobiographies are factually accurate is troubling when she considers the reliability of the authors' descriptions of the motives that prompted their career choices. Like many members of their generation (including myself, for example), the authors believe that they developed socially critical attitudes because they came to maturity during an era of significant social upheaval, witnessing such mass phenomena as the civil rights movement, protests against the Vietnam War, and the feminist movement; on an individual level, their attitudes conduced to decisions to become community psychologists, and on a collective level, their attitudes shaped the definition of community psychology as an enterprise. Certainly, generations are differentiated one from another by the experiences of their formative years, but when members of a generation describe the distinctive characteristics they possessed as young people, they may be articulating a retrospective construct, defined when a subsequent generation's values and behavior proved (somehow) disturbing. Consider, for example, Jean Ann Linney's disappointment that her students have, by contrast to members of her generation, "greater concern with professional status and identity," and less interest in "the benefits of creating alternatives or shaking up a system that they acknowledge is counterproductive." Has she succumbed to the time-worn temptation to believe that the young lack the moral virtues of their elders?

There are other reasons to suspect the authors' accounts of their career choices. Perhaps their understanding of themselves followed rather than antedated their training as community psychologists; during their professional socialization, they learned that individuals' identities are products of social forces, and came to believe that they had made their occupational choices because they were creatures of the 1960s and 1970s. Indeed, it is evident that some of the authors did not so much choose the direction they took in their careers as find themselves recruited into community psychology. Moreover, all of the authors are known to one another, joined by strong professional ties. That they tell similar stories should not be surprising. But they are surely not a skewed sample of their generation of community psychologists: in their student days, the sub-field was a small disciplinary sect, led by a few prophets.

No matter of what type (religious, political, intellectual), sects are comprised of persons joined by shared feelings of identity and purpose.

The specific biographical details provided by the authors suggest that their descriptions of their youthful selves can be trusted, however. Most of the authors acquired the perspective of distance from social conventions at very early ages, having experienced some sort of social marginality. For example, they grew up among children whose class, race, and religious backgrounds were different from theirs, and/or they were aware that their two parents came from very different backgrounds, and/or they regularly moved among distinct social worlds, learning to modify their behavior to suit the particular norms obtaining in each situation in which they found themselves. Some of them report that they were known "troublemakers" as children. A number of them had difficulties in school, ranging from the inability to do well on standardized tests, to problems with authority figures, to failure to meet academic expectations. This is not to suggest that all of the autobiographies report troubled childhoods; some of the authors were reared in relatively privileged circumstances. Nevertheless, by the time they had finished college, all of the authors had been in situations in which they were obliged to see themselves as others saw them–as members of categorical groups–to recognize that while social labeling is often arbitrary, it has real consequences for individuals. Moreover, they saw the experience of marginality in positive terms (though only Edison Trickett undertook to perpetuate it, creating a life involving regular movement between the social worlds of folk music and psychology).

Thus, the authors came to community psychology already persuaded of its fundamental assumptions by virtue of their objective circumstances. They had already achieved a critical perspective on taken-for-granted social expectations. And they were persons who were prepared to take risks because of their marginality. Thirty years ago (or so), becoming a community psychologist was risk-taking behavior. For example, Rhona Weinstein notes that young faculty could not get tenure in the program at Yale in which she was trained because their work "did not fit the mold of mainstream psychology." And searching for a job at the beginning of her career, Marybeth Shinn was told by one department chair that community psychology was "outside the field of psychology, as we define it." She should not have been surprised, for she and her colleagues were subversives in psychology, prepared to believe, for example, that amateur therapists could be more effective than professionally-trained ones (see also the memoirs of Linney and Julian Rappaport). In short, the young community psychologists' behavior fits a pattern that historians of science have often observed: disciplinary innovations are often made by marginal figures, since individuals who have consistently been rewarded for conformity to conventional standards are unlikely to violate these standards and throw in their lots with upstarts.

By definition, however, an innovative group that achieves inter-generational persistence cannot preserve its upstart character; new occupational groups endure only when they develop routine patterns of recruitment, training, certification, and practice. What was once a principled calling may become only a job. Linney, as quoted earlier, may be glorifying herself and her contemporaries at the expense of her students, but there is surely some justification for her observations. Nevertheless, because community psychology has been institutionalized as a liminal field, its practitioners may never be wholly comfortable in the academy. As Shinn observes, the community psychologist confronts resistance to her analytic approach both from standard-issue psychologists, who don't understand "why situations matter," and from standard-issue sociologists, who don't recognize the "explanatory power" of such psychological constructs as "needs." Indeed, the community psychologist may anticipate such objections by virtue of his interdisciplinary education, as N. Dickon Reppucci's recollection of his graduate training suggests. Thus, their field's structured interdisciplinarity may position community psychologists to retain the socially critical stance that has been fundamental to their enterprise.

COMMENTARY

Personal Destiny, Chance, and the Role of the Outsider in the Life Stories of Six Community Psychologists

Dan P. McAdams

Northwestern University

KEYWORDS. Narrative, identity, Community Psychologist, the outsider, serendipity, generativity, redemption

When Marybeth Shinn taught school in a rural Kenyan village in 1973, little children would sometimes burst into tears at the first sight of her. "My pale, ghostlike appearance made me almost human but not quite," she writes. She was the first white person that these children had ever seen–the ultimate *outsider* who was now *inside* the village. The vivid scene from Shinn's life story serves as a metaphor for the work and the identity of the community psychologist, as depicted in these six fascinating accounts.

Rhona Weinstein reports that growing up in an intellectual and politically-active Jewish family in Montreal, she felt like an outsider. She remembers Christians calling her a "dirty Jew," and she remembers her more bourgeois Jewish friends calling her "poor." "Even within my own group, I felt apart." Along with Shinn and Weinstein, Jean Ann Linney crossed the gender barrier of mid-century American academia. Her male colleagues may not have burst into tears at the sight of her, but they appear in some cases to have been just as puzzled as the children of Kenya. How do you act around an outsider? In Linney's first academic job, a male colleague "appeared naked during work-related interchanges." Neither the department chair nor the college dean knew how to respond to this kind of sexual harassment. Early experience prepared Julian Rappaport to be an "insider/outsider," he writes. "History has taken my autobiography to the margins." Even as a first-year graduate student, Dick Reppucci found he sympathized with those on the margins of society. At Harvard in the early 1960s, he wrote his first paper on *prostitutes*.

And, in a life story that is as much about folk singing as academia, Edison Trickett writes about crossing margins of class and culture. Enrolled in an elite preparatory school in Washington D.C., "I never transcended my feeling of marginality." In Trickett's story, folk music and community psychology are parallel worlds that nonetheless share much in common. Both settings connect Trickett "to the lives and struggles of people led in vastly different ecologies," while affirming "the uncommon strengths of common folks and the ways they accommodate to adversity with integrity." Folk singing and community psychology provide Trickett with strong feelings of community. But the one time he tried to merge the two contexts into one, he failed. In the folk concert Trickett organized for the APA's Division 27 biennial in 1987, he felt "patently outside" of both contexts, too stressed to enjoy performing in front of his psychology colleagues. Crossing boundaries is always risky, even as it offers unparalleled rewards.

In different ways, each of these life stories addresses what Mary Douglas (1966; in Shinn) described as the dangers and the rewards of *liminality*–living on the borders of known things, crossing borders and margins, knowing marginality, moving from the outside in and then back out again. By training and perhaps even by innate sentiment, community psychologists are especially attuned to the boundary between inside and outside. Community psychologists often focus their inquiries and their interventions on life at the margins: the struggles of immigrants and refugees, race relations, community mental health, homelessness. Even as children, all six authors in this volume expressed strong interest in social and political issues involving life at the margins. But community psychology as a field also enjoys something of an insider/outsider status in contemporary American psychology. Disenchanted with the mainstream approaches to be found in mid-century empirical psychology and clinical practice, the first-generation pioneers in the field of community psychology, like Seymour Sarason and Jim Kelly, envisioned an interdisciplinary enterprise focusing on the ecology of human development, social settings and contexts, and action research designed to address real social problems in communities. The field of community psychology is still new and still seen as marginal in the eyes of some traditional psychology departments. Even when they are associated with well-established programs in community psychology, therefore, community psychologists still know well what it means to be the outsider.

The person on the margins may feel that he or she has little control over where life will go. Perhaps none of us has much control in that regard, but living on the boundaries may afford a clearer view of that truth. All six authors emphasize the power of serendipity and chance in their life stories. Nobody could have predicted that they would end up being community psychologists, especially since community psychology did not even exist as a discipline when they were children. "I became a community psychologist by accident," Reppucci writes. All six authors emphasize the roles of social context and contingencies. Family settings, school experiences, religious institutions, the war in Viet-Nam, the women's movement, graduate training, a lucky break here, a mishap there, discrimination and prejudice, the inexplicable kindness of strangers and friends–so many factors in the social ecologies of these lives shaped the stories that were ultimately written and lived, stories that are still in process, still being lived. Community psychologists are trained to explain lives in terms of social contingencies, context, and the vagaries of chance, so it is not surprising that their life stories would follow these lines. "The generalized, near automatic tendency to see contextual explanations for behavior has been with me for as long as I can remember," writes Linney. "I don't know quite where this came from, but it has clearly been important in keeping me centered as a community psychologist."

Nonetheless, stories of serendipity and contextual contingencies still afford ample narrative space for human agency, and these six life stories are no exception. The authors point to important choices they made that shaped who they have become. And they often use a language of personal destiny and deep conviction that is especially compelling. This language is something that I have noted in many American life stories, but especially in those told by many midlife American men and women who score especially high on measures of what Erik Erikson (1963) called *generativity*. Generativity is the adult's concern for and commitment to promoting the well-being of future generations, through parenting, teaching, mentoring, and engaging in other life activities aimed at leaving a positive legacy of the self for the future (de St. Aubin, McAdams, & Kim, 2004; McAdams & de St. Aubin, 1998). If I might go out on a limb here, I would submit that all six of these authors are highly generative American adults who, perhaps more interestingly, are identified with a field of study and action whose goals are themselves inherently generative. In Weinstein's words, community psychology is fundamentally about "understanding and creating social settings that enhance human development." While many enterprises in life may express generative features, here we have an entire subdiscipline of psychology given over to the good work of generativity! All six of these authors see their work as something of a mission in generativity. Shinn speaks of looking for a *vocation* in life, aimed at using the gifts of one's talents and skills to "alleviate suffering" in the world. In college, Linney internalized "the expectation that each of us has a responsibility to make a difference during our lives, to contribute in some way that would leave the world a better place" for the next generation.

In ways reminiscent of the life stories that I have studied from highly generative teachers, community volunteers, and certain other midlife American men and women, these six community psychologists speak of sensing early on in life that: (1) there is suffering and injustice in the world and (2) I have special gifts or powers that will make a positive difference (McAdams, Diamond, Mansfield, & de St. Aubin, 1997). Rappaport's story is emblematic. It begins this way:

> The intersection of autobiography and history is something I have always taken for granted. My earliest memories include a father in uniform who returned from the war to die from what was called 'a service connected disability.' I never doubted that life would be lived in the context of a larger world, not an abstract larger world,

but one that is concrete, one that enters the door unbidden and takes me by the hand or by the heart to places unexpected.

For Rappaport, the story begins with a tragic setback and the sense that life is unpredictable. The young protagonist does not know where life will take him next. Yet, we soon learn that as a result of his father's death, the protagonist *does* come to know a number of things *for sure*–that he will strive to be like his father might have been, that he will go to college, that he will make a positive difference on a broad societal stage. Linney writes that "a number of childhood experiences highlighted a state of affairs in the world that seemed inherently unjust to me." Blessed by "naïve idealism, supportive contexts, and good fortune," she eventually moves herself into a position to address injustices. As a child, Trickett was moved by his grandfather's stories of coal-miners, helping him to understand "the marginality of the powerless." Repucci was embarrassed by the handouts his own impoverished family received. The authors speak of *learning early on that life is really tough, unfair, or unjust and developing resolve, often inchoate and inexpressible, to act in some manner of constructive defiance*. It takes many years to translate disappointment, loss, frustration, or outrage into redemptive action. But the move from suffering to redemption eventually occurs, even as suffering continues. In the life stories of highly generative American adults, the characters do not necessarily live happily ever after. But the stories hold hope and faith in the power of human redemption.

In conclusion, I must say that it is a pleasure to read these life-narrative accounts, and a privilege to be asked to comment upon them. Each story eloquently expresses the unique life experience of its author. As an imaginative rendering of the past and anticipation of the future, each life story, furthermore, gives us a glimpse into the complex narrative identity constructed by each of these eminent community psychologists. And each story speaks to the strength, the diversity, and the generative impact of community psychology in America today.

REFERENCES

De St. Aubin, E., McAdams, D.P., & Kim, T.C. (2004). (Eds.). *The generative society*. Washington, D.C.: APA Books.

Douglas, M. (1966). *Purity and danger: An analysis of concepts of pollution and taboo*. London: Penguin.

Erikson, E.H. (1963). *Childhood and society* (2nd Ed.). New York: Norton.

McAdams, D.P., & de St. Aubin, E. (1998). (Eds.). *Generativity and adult development: How and why we care for the next generation.* Washington, D.C.: APA Books.

McAdams, D.P., Diamond, A., de St. Aubin, E., & Mansfield, E.M. (1997). Stories of commitment: The psychosocial construction of generative lives. *Journal of Personality and Social Psychology, 72,* 678-694.

Index

Autobiographical memories
   research on, 3-4
   validity of, 149-152
Autobiography
   alternative views of, 2-3
   validity of, 2
   value of, 3

(University of) California
   at Berkeley, 125-147
   at Davis, 1-14
Catholic education, 85-87
Commentary, 153-158
Community psychology
   current context for women, 98-101
   history of, 6
Cowen, Emory L., 28-29

Feminism, 110-112

GI Bill, 19-20

History
   of community psychology, 6
   of psychology, 5

(University of) Illinois
   at Chicago, 63-80
   at Urbana-Champaign, 15-39

Kelly, James G., 1-14
Kuhn, Thomas, 1
Kuklick, Henrika, 149-152

Liminality, 154-155
Linney, Jean Ann, 6,81-102
   current context for women, 98-101
   family context, 82-85
   formative values and ideals, 82-88
   gender discrimination and, 92-93
   gender stereotype counterbalances, 87-88
   intellectual/educational context, 88-96
   intellectual identity formation, 96-98
   mentors, 93-94
   postgraduate study, 90-92
   religious education, 85-87
   scientific/intellectual context, 94-96
   undergraduate education, 88-90

Memories, validity of, 149-152
Mentors/mentoring, 23-25,28-29, 70-71,93-94

New York University, 103-124

Overview, 1-14
   historical, 5-6
   of process, 8-11
   research on memories, 3-4
   of text, 6-7
   themes, 8-11
   views on autobiography, 2-3

(University of) Pennsylvania, 149-152
Personality, 2

Psychology
   community. *See* Community psychology
   history of, 5

Rappaport, Julian, 6, 15-39, 156-157
   as assistant professor, 32-34
   community mental health/psychology, introduction to, 29-30
   dissertation, 31-32
   early (mis)education (1948-1960), 17-19
   early family life (1942-1948), 16-17
   historical context, 30-31
   marriage, 23-25
   medical school, 27-28
   mentors, 23-25, 28-29
   neighborhood (1942-1946), 20
   new neighborhood (1952-1960), 21-22
   paying for college (1960-1964), 19-20
   postgraduate study (1964-1968), 23-27
   professional experiences, 35
   public housing (1947-1952), 20-21
   public/private life intersection, 37-38
   social marginality, 38-39
   at U. Illinois post tenure, 36
   undergraduate education (1960-1964), 22-23
Reppucci, N. Dickon, 6, 41-62, 155
   discussion, 59-61
   family background, 47-50
   marriage, 52-53
   postgraduate study, 42-47
   undergraduate education, 50-52
   Virginia years, 57-59
   Yale years, 53-57

SAT scores, 18
Serendipity, 9-10

Sex discrimination, 8-9, 92-93, 110-112. *See also* Gender *entries*
Sexual harassment, 93
Shinn, Marybeth, 6, 103-124, 153-154
   diversity and, 113-114
   family background, 104-106
   family educational level, 104
   family gender roles, 105-106
   family religion, 105
   feminism and, 110-112
   future directions, 123-124
   historical context, 106-109
   postgraduate study, 114-118
   professional experience, 118-123
   sex discrimination and, 110-112
   undergraduate education, 106-114
Small truths, 10
Social-cognitive approaches, 2
Social marginality, 8-9, 38-39, 154-155
Social settings, power of, 10-11
Song, Anna V., 1-14
(University of) South Carolina, 81-102

Themes
   power of social settings, 10-11
   serendipity as, 9-10
   sex discrimination as, 8-9
   small truths, 10
   social marginality as, 8-9
   turning points, 10
Trickett, Edison J., 6, 63-80, 154, 157
   adolescence and high school, 70
   general background, 64-70
   historical context, 72
   mentors, 70-71
   postgraduate study, 73-75
   at U. Illinois, 78-80
   undergraduate education, 71-73
   at Yale, 73-78
Turning points, 10

Index

University of California
   at Berkeley, 125-147
   at Davis, 1-14
University of Illinois
   at Chicago, 63-80
   at Urbana-Champaign, 15-39
University of Pennsylvania, 149-152
University of South Carolina, 81-102
University of Virginia, 41-62

Weinstein, Rhona S., 6, 125-147, 154
   discussion, 146
   family background, 127-129
   marriage, 134-135
   postgraduate study (McGill University), 135-138
   postgraduate study (Yale), 138-142
   professional experiences, 142-145
   social environment, 129-132
   undergraduate education, 132-134

> Monographs "Separates" list continued

Prevention and School Transitions, edited by Leonard A. Jason, PhD, Karen E. Danner, and Karen S. Kurasaki, MA* (Vol. 10, No. 2, 1994). *"A collection of studies by leading ecological and systems-oriented theorists in the area of school transitions, describing the stressors, personal resources available, and coping strategies among different groups of children and adolescents undergoing school transitions." (Reference & Research Book News)*

Religion and Prevention in Mental Health: Research, Vision, and Action, edited by Kenneth I. Pargament, PhD, Kenneth I. Maton, PhD, and Robert E. Hess, PhD* (Vol. 9, No. 2 & Vol. 10, No. 1, 1992). *"The authors provide an admirable framework for considering the important, yet often overlooked, differences in theological perspectives." (Family Relations)*

Families as Nurturing Systems: Support Across the Life Span, edited by Donald G. Unger, PhD, and Douglas R. Powell, PhD* (Vol. 9, No. 1, 1991). *"A useful book for anyone thinking about alternative ways of delivering a mental health service." (British Journal of Psychiatry)*

Ethical Implications of Primary Prevention, edited by Gloria B. Levin, PhD, and Edison J. Trickett, PhD* (Vol. 8, No. 2, 1991). *"A thoughtful and thought-provoking summary of ethical issues related to intervention programs and community research." (Betty Tableman, MPA, Director, Division. of Prevention Services and Demonstration Projects, Michigan Department of Mental Health, Lansing)* Here is the first systematic and focused treatment of the ethical implications of primary prevention practice and research.

Career Stress in Changing Times, edited by James Campbell Quick, PhD, MBA, Robert E. Hess, PhD, Jared Hermalin, PhD, and Jonathan D. Quick, MD* (Vol. 8, No. 1, 1990). *"A well-organized book.... It deals with planning a career and career changes and the stresses involved." (American Association of Psychiatric Administrators)*

Prevention in Community Mental Health Centers, edited by Robert E. Hess, PhD, and John Morgan, PhD* (Vol. 7, No. 2, 1990). *"A fascinating bird's-eye view of six significant programs of preventive care which have survived the rise and fall of preventive psychiatry in the U.S." (British Journal of Psychiatry)*

Protecting the Children: Strategies for Optimizing Emotional and Behavioral Development, edited by Raymond P. Lorion, PhD* (Vol. 7, No. 1, 1990). *"This is a masterfully conceptualized and edited volume presenting theory-driven, empirically based, developmentally oriented prevention." (Michael C. Roberts, PhD, Professor of Psychology, The University of Alabama)*

The National Mental Health Association: Eighty Years of Involvement in the Field of Prevention, edited by Robert E. Hess, PhD, and Jean DeLeon, PhD* (Vol. 6, No. 2, 1989). *"As a family life educator interested in both the history of the field, current efforts, and especially the evaluation of programs, I find this book quite interesting. I enjoyed reviewing it and believe that I will return to it many times. It is also a book I will recommend to students." (Family Relations)*

A Guide to Conducting Prevention Research in the Community: First Steps, by James G. Kelly, PhD, Nancy Dassoff, PhD, Ira Levin, PhD, Janice Schreckengost, MA, AB, Stephen P. Stelzner, PhD, and B. Eileen Altman, PhD* (Vol. 6, No. 1, 1989). *"An invaluable compendium for the prevention practitioner, as well as the researcher, laying out the essentials for developing effective prevention programs in the community.... This is a book which should be in the prevention practitioner's library, to read, re-read, and ponder." (The Community Psychologist)*

Prevention: Toward a Multidisciplinary Approach, edited by Leonard A. Jason, PhD, Robert D. Felner, PhD, John N. Moritsugu, PhD, and Robert E. Hess, PhD* (Vol. 5, No. 2, 1987). *"Will not only be of intellectual value to the professional but also to students in courses aimed at presenting a refreshingly comprehensive picture of the conceptual and practical relationships between community and prevention." (Seymour B. Sarason, Associate Professor of Psychology, Yale University)*

Prevention and Health: Directions for Policy and Practice, edited by Alfred H. Katz, PhD, Jared A. Hermalin, PhD, and Robert E. Hess, PhD* (Vol. 5, No. 1, 1987). *Read about the most current efforts being undertaken to promote better health.*

The Ecology of Prevention: Illustrating Mental Health Consultation, edited by James G. Kelly, PhD, and Robert E. Hess, PhD* (Vol. 4, No. 3/4, 1987). *"Will provide the consultant with a very useful framework and the student with an appreciation for the time and commitment necessary to bring about lasting changes of a preventive nature." (The Community Psychologist)*

Beyond the Individual: Environmental Approaches and Prevention, edited by Abraham Wandersman, PhD, and Robert E. Hess, PhD* (Vol. 4, No. 1/2, 1985). *"This excellent book has immediate appeal for those involved with environmental psychology . . . likely to be of great interest to those working in the areas of community psychology, planning, and design." (Australian Journal of Psychology)*

Prevention: The Michigan Experience, edited by Betty Tableman, MPA, and Robert E. Hess, PhD* (Vol. 3, No. 4, 1985). *An in-depth look at one state's outstanding prevention programs.*

Studies in Empowerment: Steps Toward Understanding and Action, edited by Julian Rappaport, Carolyn Swift, and Robert E. Hess, PhD* (Vol. 3, No. 2/3, 1984). *"Provides diverse applications of the empowerment model to the promotion of mental health and the prevention of mental illness." (Prevention Forum Newsline)*

Aging and Prevention: New Approaches for Preventing Health and Mental Health Problems in Older Adults, edited by Sharon P. Simson, Laura Wilson, Jared Hermalin, PhD, and Robert E. Hess, PhD* (Vol. 3, No. 1, 1983). *"Highly recommended for professionals and laymen interested in modern viewpoints and techniques for avoiding many physical and mental health problems of the elderly. Written by highly qualified contributors with extensive experience in their respective fields." (Clinical Gerontologist)*

Strategies for Needs Assessment in Prevention, edited by Alex Zautra, Kenneth Bachrach, and Robert E. Hess, PhD* (Vol. 2, No. 4, 1983). *"An excellent survey on applied techniques for doing needs assessments. . . . It should be on the shelf of anyone involved in prevention." (Journal of Pediatric Psychology)*

Innovations in Prevention, edited by Robert E. Hess, PhD, and Jared Hermalin, PhD* (Vol. 2, No. 3, 1983). *An exciting book that provides invaluable insights on effective prevention programs.*

Rx Television: Enhancing the Preventive Impact of TV, edited by Joyce Sprafkin, Carolyn Swift, PhD, and Robert E. Hess, PhD* (Vol. 2, No. 1/2, 1983). *"The successful interventions reported in this volume make interesting reading on two grounds. First, they show quite clearly how powerful television can be in molding children. Second, they illustrate how this power can be used for good ends." (Contemporary Psychology)*

Early Intervention Programs for Infants, edited by Howard A. Moss, MD, Robert E. Hess, PhD, and Carolyn Swift, PhD* (Vol. 1, No. 4, 1982). *"A useful resource book for those child psychiatrists, paediatricians, and psychologists interested in early intervention and prevention." (The Royal College of Psychiatrists)*

Helping People to Help Themselves: Self-Help and Prevention, edited by Leonard D. Borman, PhD, Leslie E. Borck, PhD, Robert E. Hess, PhD, and Frank L. Pasquale* (Vol. 1, No. 3, 1982). *"A timely volume . . . a mine of information for interested clinicians, and should stimulate those wishing to do systematic research in the self-help area." (The Journal of Nervous and Mental Disease)*

Evaluation and Prevention in Human Services, edited by Jared Hermalin, PhD, and Jonathan A. Morell, PhD* (Vol. 1, No. 1/2, 1982). *Features methods and problems related to the evaluation of prevention programs.*

9780789025111